Adam Smith's Daughters

Adam Smith's Daughters

Dorothy Lampen Thomson
Herbert H. Lehman College
City University of New York

An Exposition-University Book

EXPOSITION PRESS NEW YORK

To the memory of Willis I. Thomson

EXPOSITION PRESS, INC.

50 Jericho Turnpike, Jericho, New York 11753

FIRST EDITION

LIBRARY OF CONGRESS CATALOG CARD NUMBER: 72-97724

SBN 0-682-47675-7

Published simultaneously in Canada by Transcanada Books

Contents

Preface

This is an essay on the contributions that six women have made to economics. Its purpose is to fill a void that exists in most treatises on the history of economics in which women's contributions have usually been ignored. The effort here is not only to correct this deficiency, but to remind all readers, including those who are now, or who may become economists, that six women have blazed a trail in economics and have left a rich heritage.

Early contributions to economics by women have usually been ignored or derided for two reasons: first, because their work has been appraised not within the framework of their own times, but from the perspective of twentieth-century accumulated wisdom, in the light of which they were judged naive; and second, because they did not think like men. Here their writings are viewed within the context of their own times and they have been permitted to speak for themselves in order to demonstrate their ability to write and to think like intelligent humans.

In my own quest for economic understanding to produce a work of this kind I have incurred many diverse debts to former teachers, colleagues, students, and friends, to whom I say "thank you." I am grateful to Thornton Wilder for his gracious permission to quote the epigraphs from *The Skin of Our Teeth* that head the several chapters. I feel and express special gratitude to two scholars: Professor Margaret Grennan Lehmann and Professor Paul Marer, each of whom has read my manuscript and has provided encouragement and invaluable suggestions for its improvement. The errors and inadequacies that remain are mine. But most especially, I thank the six women whose contributions to economics are recorded in the pages that follow.

D.L.T.

ADAM SMITH'S DAUGHTERS

Introduction

Adam Smith, a confirmed bachelor, is generally known to have had numerous "sons." Much less is known about his "daughters." While there is no record that Adam Smith ever married, nor a suggestion here or elsewhere that he was promiscuous, we are all in a sense his progeny and beneficiaries. During the two centuries since *The Wealth of Nations* was published in 1776, Adam Smith's intellectual offspring—mostly male—have been intent on designing and interpreting a society in which they, their fellows, their womenfolk, and their successors might survive and prosper. They have labored variously and well.

During these two centuries at least six remarkable women have made significant contributions to the development of economics and to the societies in which they lived. Yet one reads innumerable histories of economic thought today and learns little or nothing about several of them. In some they are derided; in others, ignored. As for the earliest of them, the profession has barely acknowledged their existence. It is about these distinguished "daughters" and "granddaughters" of Adam Smith that the following pages relate: Jane Haldimand Marcet (1769-1858), Harriet Martineau (1802-1876), Millicent Garrett Fawcett (1847-1929), Rosa Luxemburg (1870-1919), Beatrice Potter Webb (1858-1943), and Joan V. Robinson (1903-   ).

The first three, Jane Marcet, Harriet Martineau, and Millicent Fawcett, wrote on the subject tentatively when economics was still in the chrysalis stage of development. They were ardent free enterprisers. Their ideology of individualism and the literary forms

3

within which they worked inspired them to purvey simple moral precepts. Economics, in their view, had a close kinship to the moral philosophy from which it derived. The kind of philosophy that would give origin to *The Theory of Moral Sentiments* as a precursor to *The Wealth of Nations*[1] was congenial to them.

The last three, Rosa Luxemburg, Beatrice Webb, and Joan Robinson, were all collectivists in varying degrees. They were drawn to socialism in the belief that "socialism is, at its root, the effort to find a remedy in social terms for the affront to reason and morality in the status quo."[2] They wrote on economics with vigor and emphasis by reason of their own special endowments, their fortuitous timing, and their deep conviction that economics, however scientific, can never be divorced from normative propositions dictated by concern for social welfare.

A common denominator that distinguishes these women is that all six have been identified with economic education, although only limited career opportunities were available in this field for the first three. Each recognized the need for widespread economic understanding and here Jane Marcet was a true pioneer as she provided instructional materials for early day students and teachers of political economy. Harriet Martineau was an early experimenter in new techniques of adult education. Millicent Fawcett, while serving as amanuensis for her famous husband, recognized the need for making economics more comprehensible to young persons. Her concise manuals were prototypes for the many programmed study guides that abound today.

Instructional opportunities for women increased with time. Rosa Luxemburg was a lecturer on political economy for five years in the Social Democratic party training school in Berlin. Beatrice Webb helped to found and lectured for many years in the prestigious London School of Economics. Joan Robinson, an inspiring teacher at the University of Cambridge for over forty years as well as a highly productive and respected scholar, is one of the leaders in the profession. Hers is the only contribution to economics made by a woman that is cited in a recent list of sixty-two outstanding achievements in the behavioral and social sciences since 1900. After delivering the Richard T. Ely lecture on the topic

The Second Crisis of Economic Theory at the annual meeting of the American Economic Association in December 1971, she received a standing ovation by an overflow audience of her fellow professionals.

The concern of all six for moral teaching contrasts with the mechanistic approach of a majority of modern economists who would have their profession shun value judgments as they concentrate on developing a " 'kit of tools' for the examination or repair of the existing social mechanism."[3] Yet we find kindred spirits among the moderns.

John Kenneth Galbraith wrote in *The Affluent Society* while fulminating against "the conventional wisdom": "Once students were attracted [to economics] by the seeming urgency of economic problems and by a sense of their mission to solve them. Now the best come to economics for the opportunity it provides to exercise arcane mathematical skills." To this Galbraith added: "Much more than decisions on economic policy are involved. A system of morality is at stake. . . . The central or classical tradition of economics was more than an analysis of economic behavior and a set of rules for economic polity. It also had a moral code."[4]

Kenneth E. Boulding, in his 1968 presidential address to the American Economic Association, stated: ". . . no science of any kind can be divorced from ethical considerations. . . . We cannot escape the proposition that as science moves from pure knowledge toward control, that is, toward creating what it knows, what it creates becomes a problem of ethical choice, and will depend upon the common values of the societies in which the scientific subculture is embedded. . . . Under these circumstances science cannot proceed at all without at least an implicit ethic, that is a subculture with appropriate common values."[5]

Robert L. Heilbroner, emphasizing the connectedness of economic and noneconomic processes, wrote in 1970: "By divorcing itself from the need to strugggle with the elements of the political and social world, however recalcitrant they may be, conventional economics has ensured its technical virtuosity and its internal consistency, but at the cost of its social relevance."[6]

The six women whose work is presented in the following

pages would affirm strongly both the moral responsibility and the need for social relevance which, according to Galbraith, Boulding, and Heilbroner, economists should never ignore.

Yet these women did not confine themselves to economic education. Instead, each viewed her subject in larger context and identified with problems of current significance. Three of the six (Millicent Fawcett, Rosa Luxemburg, Beatrice Webb) engaged actively in politics. Jane Marcet became a prolific writer of educational materials for children on a great variety of subjects other than economics; Harriet Martineau became a perceptive and influential journalist; Millicent Fawcett became a leader in the women's rights movement. Rosa Luxemburg, caught up by Marx's tempestuous challenge to classical orthodoxy, spearheaded study of the economic foundations of imperialism and became an eloquent spokesman for Marxism. Beatrice Webb devoted her talents to exploring the origin and role of certain social institutions, such as consumer cooperation and trade unions, and to learning the causes and solving the problem of why poverty afflicts so many able-bodied persons. As social investigator and member of government commissions she viewed the appropriate focus of social inquiry not as a quest for wealth but as a "war on poverty"—a phrase which appears in her dairy in 1912. Early in her career Joan Robinson came to the conclusion that static economic theory was barren. Thus she made important contributions first in micro- and then in macroeconomics, urging her fellow economists to seek relevance by increasing their awareness of the real world of continuous change.

The interests of these six women—education, imperialism, women's rights, war on poverty, trade unionism, breakthroughs in micro- and macroeconomic theory—could scarcely contain a livelier list of modern topics occupying the concern of economists today, for which one or another of these women provided an initial or an early spark. Viewed in sequence their work provides a capsule history of economic thought—a fitting counterpoint to the work of Adam Smith's sons.

NOTES

1. See Ralph Anspach, "The Implications of the *Theory of Moral Sentiments* for Adam Smith's Economic Thought" in *History of Political Economy* (Spring, 1972), 4:1, 176-206.
2. Robert L. Heilbroner, *Between Capitalism and Socialism* (New York: Vintage Books, 1970), p. 113.
3. Ibid. p. xii.
4. John Kenneth Galbraith, *The Affluent Society* (Boston: Houghton Mifflin, 1958), pp. 142, 289.
5. Kenneth E. Boulding, "Economics as a Moral Science," *American Economic Review* (March 1969), LIX: 2, 3.
6. Heilbroner, op. cit., p. xiii.

CHAPTER I

Jane Haldimand Marcet
(1769-1858)

"As for me, I don't understand a single word of it, anyway,—all about the troubles the human race has gone through, there's a subject for you."
—Thornton Wilder, *The Skin of Our Teeth**

Early nineteenth-century England was not a propitious time or place for a woman to become an economist. Economics was still neither a scholarly nor a popular study. It had, in fact, only recently gained respectability. In the opinion of the seventeenth century and much of the eighteenth century, the study of trade was beneath the dignity of learning, and the view that "the gentleman does not sully his hands in trade" was one that was slow to be overcome. The science of economics had been born outside the universities, without the blessing of the academic scholars. The prevailing view was that "no gentleman, and especially no self-respecting scholar, would study the profession if he were not forced to."[1] The universities had barely given lip service to the subject by viewing it, first, in terms of Aristotle's "Economica"— a study limited to the nature and management of the household —and later, as a branch of moral philosophy. "Up to 1818," said a writer in the *Westminster Review,* "the subject was scarcely discussed outside a small circle of philosophers."[2]

Moreover, the political and economic emancipation of women was still a century away. The drive for educational equality of

---

*The quotations from *The Skin of Our Teeth* are reprinted by special permission of Thornton Wilder.

women had scarcely begun. At a time when it was considered unfeminine for women to show that they have brains it required courage for anyone to attempt to break the mold. Yet, in 1816, Jane Haldimand Marcet undertook "to bring within the reach of young persons a science which no English writer has yet presented in an easy and familiar form."[3] Thereupon, she became the first woman to become identified with the science of economics—or political economy as it was originally known—and the first person seriously to undertake the task of economic education.

Jane Haldimand Marcet's long life overlapped the lives of all the classical economists, from Adam Smith to Alfred Marshall. Although she was to know only some of them personally, she became well aware of the growing interest and importance of political economy during her lifetime. One of twelve children, most of whom died in infancy or early childhood, she was the only surviving daughter of a wealthy Swiss merchant who had located in London and later founded a banking house. We know little of her parents, her early life, or education, but there is evidence that she grew up in a secure home that was actively involved with contemporary economic ideas and affairs. At a time when most education was given at home, boys and girls were exposed to it equally, but girls were expected to stay at home and be "feminine," while boys were thrust into the world at an early age. Her younger brother, William Haldimand (1784-1862) received "a plain English education," entered his father's counting house at sixteen, showed great talent for the business, and became a director of the Bank of England at twenty-five.[4] Later in this capacity and as a Member of Parliament for Ipswich, he was examined in February 1819 for two days successively and for five hours each day by a Lords Committee on the resumption of cash payments by the Bank of England, "and the effect produced by his evidence and the information he had given the Committee was a subject of general remark and congratulation."[5] No doubt Jane Haldimand's education, formally under governesses and tutors, consisted largely of intellectual stimulation from a cultured home and a multiplicity of activities patterned according to the current customs and education that aimed to produce the polite accomplishments appropriate to the daughter of a wealthy upper-middle-class family of the time. No doubt, too, she was exposed to frequent discussion of current economic topics.

Jane married Swiss-born Dr. Alexander John Gaspard Marcet (1770-1822) in 1799 at the age of thirty. He had received a medical degree from the University of Edinburgh two years before. In addition to establishing a private practice in London, Dr. Marcet delivered lectures in chemistry at Guy's Hospital, and published medical and chemical papers. He belonged to the Geological Society of London of which David Ricardo was a prominent member.[6] Dr. Marcet retired from his medical practice in 1819, and he and his wife went to live in Geneva where he became a professor of chemistry. There is evidence[7] that the Marcets and David Ricardo were socially friendly, with Mr. Ricardo dining at the Marcets' in February 1819 before their departure for Switzerland, and years later Mrs. Marcet was included among those who had "breakfasts at Mr. Ricardo's."[8] Dr. Marcet's death, on a visit to London in 1822, left Jane a widow at fifty-three; she was to live to eighty-nine.

Why did Jane Haldimand Marcet become the first woman to be identified with economics? Most likely, by a combination of events rather than by deliberate design. Jane Marcet's family background and her marriage to a scientist-teacher were two major influences that probably determined the course of her life. In addition, she lived during an era when there was a growing interest in the movement for economic independence and educational equality of women, the incipience of which paralleled her own girlhood. As a young woman, Jane Haldimand would certainly have known of the exceptional career of Mary Wollstonecraft, a fellow resident of London and Jane's senior by only ten years who, more than any other person, was responsible for initiating this movement.[9]

In the five years between 1787 and 1792 Mary Wollstonecraft (later Mrs. William Godwin, 1759-1797) wrote a remarkable sequence of books, any one of which might have aroused serious ambitions for a literary career in the mind of young Jane Haldimand. The first of these, *Thoughts on the Education of Daughters:*

with Reflections on Female conduct, in the More Important Duties of Life was a potpourri of twenty-one short essays having no unity or organization, but with a thesis that women were being ill prepared for life, and a plea for their intellectual improvement. This was followed in 1788 by *Original Stories from Real Life; with Conversations, Calculated to Regulate the Affections, and Form the Mind to Truth and Goodness.* This was a collection of stories for children that concerned two girls, Mary and Caroline, who had been placed by their father under the care and instruction of a widowed relative, Mrs. Mason, who undertook her task with intense seriousness devoid of any humor. Such old-fashioned virtues as humility, charity, fortitude, piety, promptness, and industry were extolled by precept and example. Whether or not the book pleased young readers, it appealed to their parents. It met with immediate success, appearing in successive editions in both London and Dublin, and continued in popularity well into the 1830s.

In 1789 Mary Wollstonecraft compiled an anthology, *The Female Reader; or Miscellaneous Pieces, in Prose and Verse; Selected from the Best Writers, and Disposed under Proper Heads; for the Improvement of Young Women.* Although this was not an original work, except for the "Preface; containing some Hints on Female Education," yet it and her previous publications were important prolegomena for her original and most famous work, *A Vindication of the Rights of Woman* which appeared in 1792.[10] This work "was to prove her the most fearlessly intelligent woman of her time—and perhaps the greatest."[11] Herein, with fire and acrimony, she deplored the empty, "insulated" pattern of women's lives, condemned their "disorderly kind of education," and pleaded for coeducational schooling. She stated in her introduction that she had arrived at "a profound conviction that the neglected education of my fellow-creatures is the grand source of the misery I deplore." She argued that women deserve equality with men and should be given the education necessary to achieve it. She wrote: "In order to open their faculties they should be excited to think for themselves; and this can only be done by mixing a number of children together, and making them jointly pursue the same objects."[12]

Mary Wollstonecraft urged a kind of education that would provide a "free use of reason" to "make women rational creatures and free citizens."[13] She recommended a curriculum that would include "botany, mechanics, and astronomy; reading, writing, arithmetic, natural history, and some simple experiments in natural philosophy,"[14] and added: "The elements of religion, history, the history of men, and politics, might also be taught by conversations in the Socratic form."[15] This sentence, possibly more than any other,* may have fired the youthful Jane Marcet's imagination to undertake what was to become her life work.

Mrs. Marcet soon began to write books of Socratic dialogue on every subject Mary Wollstonecraft had suggested should be included in the education of young persons. With some temerity, she began writing on a subject on which her husband could provide expert guidance and criticism. *Conversations on Chemistry, in which the Elements of that Science are Familiarly Explained, and Illustrated by Experiments* was published anonymously in two volumes in 1806. (Not only were elaborate titles typical of the period, but it was customary throughout the eighteenth century and after for authors to publish their works anonymously in order to avoid a charge of special pleading.)[16] The subject matter of *Conversations on Chemistry* was presented in twenty-six lessons and was "intended more especially for the Female sex." Its immediate and unexpected success, which reached sixteen editions during her lifetime, gave encouragement to Mrs. Marcet to continue with other subjects.

Ten years later, in 1816,—the author was then forty-seven—

---

*It is true that Mary Wollstonecraft was not alone in her awareness of the need for educational reform in behalf of women. Others, both before and after her, wrote on the same theme. Mary Wollstonecraft acknowledged indebtedness to Catherine Macaulay for her ideas expressed in *Letters on Education*. In 1795, in *Letters to Literary Ladies* and in several works thereafter, Maria Edgeworth presented a thoughtful plea and blueprint for female education. But it is more than plausible that Mary Wollstonecraft's book and the sentence quoted above provided the seminal inspiration from which Jane Marcet's life work was to grow.

Conversations on Political Economy, in which the Elements of that Science are Familiarly Explained was published. Again her authorship was concealed, and recorded only as "the Author of Conversations in Chemistry." Nevertheless, this book established her reputation as an author and educator, and thereafter a great outpouring[17] of other conversations, lessons, and stories for young children by Mrs. Marcet appeared on an amazing variety of subjects.* Two later works, which dealt with economics, *John Hopkins's Notions on Political Economy* (1833) and *Rich and Poor* (1851), will be commented on in greater detail hereafter.

Even though she had undertaken the task hesitantly, *Conversations on Political Economy* promptly became and remained Mrs. Marcet's most famous book. "Political Economy," she wrote in her preface, "though so immediately connected with the happiness and improvement of mankind, and the object of so much controversy and speculation among men of knowledge, is not yet become a popular science, and is not generally considered as a study essential to early education."[18]

Mrs Marcet needed but two fictitious characters to bring her subject to life: the pupil, Caroline—of indeterminable age, sometimes naive, often precocious, always tractable; and her teacher—dogmatic, didactic, loquacious Mrs. B. The literary historian may wonder whether the choice of the pupil's name was a grateful gesture to the earlier Caroline of Mary Wollstonecraft's *Original Stories*. And a modern reader wonders: Was Mrs. B. fashioned according to the model set by Mary Wollstonecraft's Mrs. Mason? or was she Mrs. Marcet herself? Together, in twenty-two conversations extending to four-hundred and eighty pages, they explored

---

*Conversations on Natural Philosophy, an Exposition of the First Elements of Science for Very Young Children, one of the subjects specifically named by Mary Wollstonecraft, was published in 1819. It was originally planned as an introduction to her work on chemistry and had been written before either of her former publications. A few among her many other titles were: *Conversations on Evidences of Christianity* (1826), *Conversations on Vegetable Physiology* (1829), *Conversations for Children, on Land and Water* (1838), *Conversations on the History of England* (1842), *Conversations on Language for Children* (1844).

such topics as the right of private property, capital, wages, population, rent, interest, value and price, money and foreign trade. Each conversation was interspersed with a great deal of homely philosophy and many lengthy digressions of slight relevance to political economy.

The author admitted it had been a matter of doubt among her literary advisers whether the form of dialogues should be used for presenting political economy. She decided upon it but stated that she made no effort to maintain consistency of character or intellect in the remarks of her pupil. In the persons of both Mrs. B. and Caroline the author reflects her own groping to understand her subject when she states that her method "gave her an opportunity of introducing objections, and placing in various points of view questions and answers as they had actually occurred to her own mind . . .".[19]

As her first task, Mrs. B. found that she had to overcome "a sort of antipathy to political economy"[20] on the part of her student. (What teacher of Introductory Economics today has not met with similar resistance?!) She dealt with it, after an opening discussion on the geographical division of labor ("interdependence of towns and country"), in the following dialogue:[21]

> MRS. B.   . . . you cannot well understand this question without some knowledge of the principles of political economy.
> CAROLINE.   I am very sorry to hear that, for I confess that I have a sort of antipathy to political economy.
> MRS. B.   Are you sure that you understand what is meant by political economy?
> CAROLINE.   I believe so, as it is very often the subject of conversation at home; but it appears to me the most uninteresting of all subjects. It is about custom-houses, and trade, and taxes, and bounties, and smuggling, and paper-money, and the bullion-committee, etc. which I cannot hear named without yawning. Then there is a perpetual reference to the works of Adam Smith, whose name is never uttered without such veneration, that I was induced one day to look into his work on Political Economy to gain some information on the subject of corn, but what with forestalling, regrating, duties, drawbacks, and limiting prices, I was so overwhelmed by a jargon of unintelligible terms, that after running over a few pages I

threw the book away in despair, and resolved to eat my bread in humble ignorance. So if our argument respecting town and country relates to political economy, I fancy that I must be contented to yield the point in dispute without understanding it.

MRS. B.   Well, then, if you can remain satisfied with your ignorance of political economy you should at least make up your mind to forbear from talking of it, since you cannot do it to any purpose.

CAROLINE.   I assure you that requires very little effort; I only wish that I was as certain of never hearing the subject mentioned as I am of never talking upon it myself.

MRS. B.   Do you recollect how heartily you laughed at poor Mr. Jourdain in the *Bourgeois Gentilhomme,* when he discovered that he had been speaking in prose all his life without knowing it?—Well, my dear, you frequently talk of political economy without knowing it. But a few days since I heard you deciding on the very question of the scarcity of corn; and it must be confessed that your verdict was in perfect unison with your present profession of ignorance.

CAROLINE.   Indeed I only repeated what I had heard from very sensible people, that the farmers had a great deal of corn; that if they were compelled to bring it to market there would be no scarcity, and that they kept it back with a view to their own interest, in order to raise the price. Surely it does not require a knowledge of political economy to speak on so common, so interesting a subject as this first necessary of life.

MRS. B.   The very circumstance of its general interest renders it one of the most important branches of political economy. Unfortunately for your resolution, this science spreads into so many ramifications that you will seldom hear a conversation amongst liberal-minded people without some reference to it. It was but yesterday that you accused the Birmingham manufacturers of cruelty and injustice towards their workmen, and asserted that the rate of wages should be proportioned by law to that of provisions; in order that the poor might not be sufferers by a rise in the price of bread. I dare say you thought that you had made a very rational speech when you so decided?

CAROLINE.   And was I mistaken? You begin to excite my curiosity, Mrs. B.; do you think I shall ever be tempted to study this science?

MRS B.   I do not know; but I have no doubt that I shall convince you of your incapacity to enter on most subjects of general conversation, whilst you remain in total ignorance of it; and that however guarded you may be, that ignorance will be betrayed, and may frequently expose you to ridicule. During the riots of Nottingham I recollect hearing you condemn the invention of machines, which, by abridging labour, threw a number of workmen out of employment. Your opinion was founded upon mistaken principles of benevolence. In short, my dear, so many things are more or less connected with the science of political economy, that if you persevere in your resolution, you might almost as well condemn yourself to perpetual silence.

CAROLINE.   I should at least be privileged to talk about dress, amusements, and such lady-like topics.

MRS. B.   I have heard no trifling degree of ignorance of political economy betrayed in a conversation on dress. . . . The science of political economy is intimately connected with the daily occurrences of life, and in this respect differs materially from that of chemistry, astronomy, or any of the natural sciences; the mistakes we may fall into in the latter sciences can have little sensible effect upon our conduct, whilst our ignorance of the former may lead us into serious practical errors. . . .

CAROLINE.   Well, after all, Mrs. B., ignorance of political economy is a very excusable deficiency in women. It is the business of Government to reform the prejudices and errors which prevail respecting it; and as we are never likely to become legislators, is it not just as well that we should remain in happy ignorance of evils which we have no power to remedy?

MRS. B.   When you plead in favour of ignorance, there is a strong presumption that you are in the wrong. If a more general knowledge of political economy prevented women from propagating errors respecting it, in the education of their children, no trifling good would ensue. Childhood is spent in acquiring ideas, adolescence in discriminating and rejecting those which are false; how greatly we should facilitate this labour by diminishing the number of errors imbibed in early youth, and by inculcating such ideas only as are founded in truth.

CAROLINE.   Surely you would not teach political economy to children?

MRS. B.   I would wish that mothers were so far competent to teach it, that their children should not have any thing to unlearn; . . .

Thereafter Caroline, in a thoroughly subdued and receptive mood, humbly asked:

> Well, my dear Mrs. B., what must I do? You know that I am fond of instruction, and that I am not afraid of application. You may recollect what pleasure I took in the study of chemistry. If you could persuade me that political economy would be as interesting, and not more difficult, I would beg of you to put me in the way of learning it. Are there any lectures given on this subject? or could one take lessons of a master? . . .

> MRS. B.   . . . It is not in my power to recommend you a master on this subject, for there are none—perhaps because there are no pupils. Those who seek for instruction on political economy, read the works written on that science, particularly the treatise of Adam Smith. Lectures on political economy have occasionally been given at the universities, especially at Edinburgh, and many of the students there are well versed in this science . . .

Now, in the role of Mrs. Marcet's alter ego, Mrs. B. offered her services as teacher.

> Perhaps I may be able to smooth the way for you, It has been my good fortune to have passed a great part of my life in a society where this science has been a frequent topic of discussion, and the interest I took in it has induced me to study its principles in the works of the best writers on the subject; . . .

Thereupon the author launched on an undertaking to explain that science that "treats especially of the means of promoting social happiness so far as relates to the acquisition, possession, and use of the objects which constitute national wealth."[22] The reader is provided with explanations of many facets of political economy as the subject was understood in 1816, and in some passages we can foresee the direction that later economic inquiry was to take.

Mrs. Marcet acknowledged that she had drawn heavily on the

writings of the great masters such as Adam Smith, Malthus, Say, Sismondi, and Ricardo.[23] She accepted their ideas, quoted their words uncritically, and displayed a general complacency with the *status quo* of economic society. Doubtless, her noncritical eclecticism was responsible for extending many economic fallacies far beyond their time. Yet we are provided with many authentic economic vignettes. For example, she discusses the origins of savings banks in Scotland and is alert to their importance.[24] She tells us: "The average profits of the use of capital may be estimated at about double the interest of money. Legal interest, that is to say, the highest rate which the law allows to be given, is five per cent, and the usual profits of trade are about ten per cent."[25]

She explored in great detail the relative importance of agriculture and manufacturing, and declined to hold either mercantilism or Physiocracy in disfavor as she gave approval to industry. She concluded: "Agriculture, manufactures, and commerce, are all essential to the wellbeing of a country; and the question is not whether an exclusive preference should be given to any one of these branches of industry, but what are the proportions which they should bear to each other, in order to conduce most to the prosperity of the community."[26]

After a discussion of resource allocation and the principle of substitution, Caroline asks: "Then the profits of agriculture and manufactures will always be, or at least tend to be, upon a footing of equality?"[27] Mrs. B. discusses the tendency toward uniformity of profits and concludes: "It is thus that the distribution of capital to the several branches of agriculture, manufactures, and trade, preserve a due equilibrium."[28]

The author's discussion of the theory of value, reflecting Adam Smith's vacillation on that topic, finally concluded: "The price of a commodity, therefore, must be sufficient to defray the cost of production . . . . Thus you see that the value of a commodity is composed of three parts, rent, profit, and wages; the rent of the proprietor of land, the profits of the several employers of the capital, and the wages of the various labourers who give it qualities which render it an object of desire, and consequently a salable commodity."[29]

Throughout the *Conversations* the thesis of the importance of universal education recurs: "I know therefore of no other remedy to this evil [poverty] than the slow and gradual effect of education."[30] But the mysteries of political economy were advisedly to be dispensed cautiously—to children, yes; to labourers, no; because "knowledge in this instance [the effect of price changes on real wages] would only teach them [the labourers] that they must bear with patience an unavoidable evil."[31] Caroline asks: "Surely you would not teach political economy to the labouring classes, Mrs. B.?" And Mrs. B. replies: "No; but I would endeavor to give the rising generation such an education as would render them not only moral and religious, but industrious, frugal, and provident. . . ."[32]

The topic of Caroline's question was to become one of active controversy during the years that followed,[33] and Mrs. Marcet was to reverse her own position on this point by 1833. In that year she published *John Hopkins's Notions on Political Economy,* a collection of nine original stories on economic themes—wages, population, prices, foreign trade, machinery—which were intended "for the improvement of the laboring classes."[34] Economic topics were not treated as comprehensively in this publication as in the *Conversations,* but it gains by having better continuity. John Hopkins was a poor laborer who supported a large family on very meager wages. He had a simple, inquiring mind, less disciplined than Caroline's. He held many distorted views on economics which the stories aimed to correct. Some of the stories are delightfully told, with rapid development of sequence and lively exchange of conversation, although with minimal characterization.

The first story, "The Rich and the Poor," results from John's complaint to a fairy that "rich men by their extravagance, deprive us poor men of bread."[35] It relates the disastrous consequences due to loss of employment and markets that befell John and his friends following the destruction of all luxuries. In the second story, "Wages," John asked the fairy to double all wages. The consequent effect of calamitous inflation on prices and employment proved to John that such an act was "full of danger and mischief" and that he should "never more apply to the Fairy."[36]

The third story, the allegory of "The Three Giants," is the most effective in the collection and survives in children's story collections today. The narrator, an itinerant peddler, was to receive a night's lodging as his reward if he pleased each member of his audience. Accordingly, he sought to satisfy the wishes of each member of John Hopkins's family, one of whom requested a true story; another a story about giants or fairies; a third, a story with a moral. He told how a small group of shipwrecked islanders discovered three kind and powerful giants—slow but dependable Aquafluentes (stream of running water), fickle Ventosus (wind), and Vaparoso (steam), the truant who needed to be tamed. The three giants proved to be willing and productive helpers who "worked without board, food or wages"[37] as they ground corn, sawed lumber, wove cotton into cloth, and accomplished astonishing amounts of work. Lucid explanations of the principles of exchange, capital formation, commerce, and real wealth are subtly woven into the tale.

The author leaves the realm of fantasy with these three stories, and the economic topics developed in the remaining stories are best revealed by the alternate title assigned to each:

Population, etc.; or, The Old World.
Emigration; or, A New World.
The Poor's Rate; or, The Treacherous Friend.
Machinery; or, Cheap Goods and Dear Goods.
Foreign Trade or, The Wedding Gown.
The Corn Trade; or, The Price of Bread.

The above titles give evidence that Mrs. Marcet sought to interest not only male readers but also readers from the distaff side of the household. Although undeniably patronizing, her democratic philosophy and her belief in general education are revealed in the following passage wherein she endowed not only John Hopkins, but all her readers, with dignity and stature.

Then observing the landlord smile, "You may think, perhaps," added he [John Hopkins], twirling his hat in his hands, "that I ought to be minding my own concerns, and not troubling my head about what is above my capacity."

"I am very far from thinking," said the landlord, "that it is not your business to reflect and consider what is or what is not good for your country. It is not only the right but the duty of every free-born Englishman to do so to the best of his abilities. This, thank God, is not a land in which we are afraid of the people learning to distinguish between right and wrong, even in matters which concern the welfare of the country."[38]

The stories in *John Hopkins's Notions on Political Economy* evolved naturally from questions raised and topics discussed by Caroline and Mrs. B. in the *Conversations*. The theme of "The Three Giants," for example, had been anticipated in the *Conversations* by Mrs. B's statement that "The great efficacy of machinery in the hands of man depends upon the art of compelling natural agents, such as wind, steam, and water, to perform the task which he would otherwise be obliged to execute himself; by which means labour is very much abridged, a great deal of human effort is saved, and the work is often accomplished in a more uniform and accurate manner."[39]

Mrs. Marcet's third and last economic publication, *Rich and Poor* (1851), is also anticipated by a passage in the *Conversations*. Therein Mrs. B. had stated: "The rich and poor are necessary to each other; it is precisely the fable of the belly and the limbs; without the rich the poor would starve; without the poor the rich would be compelled to labour for their own subsistence."[40] (There is no explanation why this would be so great a calamity.) The theme is reiterated in the Preface to *Rich and Poor:* "These Dialogues," the author wrote, "contain a few of the first principles of Political Economy, and are intended for the use of children, whether rich or poor. No portion of that science is more important to the lower classes, as it teaches them that the Rich are their friends—not their foes; that to love and assist each other in all the concerns of life contributes to the happiness of both classes, and to revere the laws of God, which, whether we study them in natural science or by the help of revelation, are all directed to this end."[41] Here we find no advocacy of social reform. Mrs. Marcet was content to accept unquestioningly the stratifications of the social order and to interpret the *status quo* as she knew it.

The setting in this small seventy-five-page work was a school in a country village, taught by a popular master, Mr. B., who undertook to teach political economy to a group of six eager boys who "assented . . . with alacrity, though they did not know what it was; but they liked all he taught them." The topics of labor, profits, capital, wages, machinery, price, trade, money, and banks are treated in thirteen lessons. At the outset Mr. B. said to his pupils: "You are ignorant of the meaning of Political Economy, nor is it necessary that you should learn much of so difficult a science. I shall therefore teach you only that part most essential for you to know, which treats of the connection between different classes of mankind, that is, between the rich and the poor."[42] He continued: Rich and poor are but vague terms. In order to distinguish them better, let us call the *rich* all those who are able to live without manual labour; *manual* labour means labour of the *hands,* but in manual labour is included all bodily labour whatever [i.e. mind and body]. Poor, we will call those who are indebted to manual labour for their subsistence."[43]

Here we find the continuing confusion over the theory of wages that characterized the early writings of the classical school, but by 1851 the wages-fund doctrine had firmly replaced "the iron law of wages." The boys were told that profits were "to the advantage of all parties." They were needed to compensate for waiting and risk. The boys accepted the reasoning grudgingly, as one of them remarked: "That's the way that the rich grow richer and richer, while the poor labourer finds it a hard matter to make all ends meet."[44] After some instruction, the boys reflected: "a strange sort of a study, this political economy. . . . It seems to belong to or have to do with every thing, and that you think you know it before you are taught it; and then, when you begin to learn it, you find you are all in the wrong, and know nothing about it."[45]

Doubtless reflecting her own frustration in this student plaint, this frank admission of confusion is more commendable on the part of the author, in the light of present perspective, than the complacency expressed by her contemporary, John Stuart Mill, who, in the five essays he wrote between 1829 and 1830 and published later under the titles: *Essays on Some Unsettled Questions of Political Economy,* implied that all questions of importance except the few he discussed, had been resolved.

It is easy now for us to be critical of doctrinal inaccuracies, to regret omissions, to scoff at vacillations and contradictions, to smile condescendingly at the author's naïveté, and to be impatient with her verbosity and discursiveness. Mostly these deficiencies reflect the insecure state of economic knowledge, her awesome respect for that science, and the popular style of writing of the time. She begged indulgence of her critics and gave evidence that she was all too aware of her own deficiencies when she wrote: "It will immediately be perceived by those to whom the subject is not new, that a few of the most abstruse questions and controversies in Political Economy have been entirely omitted, and that others have been stated and discussed without any positive conclusion being deduced. This is a defect unavoidably attached not only to the author's limited knowledge, but also to the real difficulty of the science. In general, however, when the soundness of a doctrine has appeared well established, it has been stated conscientiously, without any excess of caution or reserve, and with the sole object of diffusing useful truths."[46]

Mrs. Marcet's contemporaries acknowledged that her work had made the subject popular. Writing in March 1822, Maria Edgeworth described breakfasts at Mr. Ricardo's and wrote: "It has now become high fashion with blue ladies to talk political economy. There is a certain Lady Mary Shepherd who makes a great jabbering on the subject, while others who have more sense, like Mrs. Marcet, hold their tongues and listen. . . . Mean time fine ladies now require that their daughters' governesses should teach political economy."[47]

High ranking critics also acclaimed her work. Lord Macaulay wrote in 1825 that "Every girl who has read Mrs. Marcet's little dialogues on political economy could teach Montagu or Walpole many lessons in finance."[48] J. R. McCulloch, the great popularizer of Ricardian economics and himself the author of books, articles, and tracts on political economy, wrote in 1845 that Mrs. Marcet's book is "on the whole perhaps the best introduction to the science that has yet appeared."[49] Jean Baptiste Say, the progenitor of Say's Law and the author of the *Traité d'Economie Politique,* a popular French text, gave Mrs. Marcet the grudging compliment that she was "the only woman who has written on political economy and shown herself superior even to men."[50]

Admittedly, Mrs. Marcet added nothing of doctrinal substance to economic science. In fact, by the very success of her venture,* she probably extended economic fallacies beyond their time, although in this she was not alone, nor had the fallacies originated with her. She supported the ideology of laissez faire unquestioningly. She confirmed the opinion, held by all classical economists except Malthus, in the validity of Say's Law of Markets.† (It was more than a century before the fallacies imbedded in this simplistic dogma were challenged effectively.) And the modern reader winces with embarrassment at her lack of social enlightenment.

Yet her identity as a pioneer in economic education should never be ignored. Mrs. Marcet gave evidence of her own awareness of this when she wrote: "the author flatters herself that this attempt will not be too severely judged. She hopes it will be remembered that in devising the plan of this work she was in a great degree obliged to form the path she has pursued, and had scarcely any other guide in this popular mode of viewing the subject, than the recollection of the impressions she herself experienced when she first turned her attention to this study; . . ."[51]

Fully aware of the importance of her task, Mrs. Marcet did indeed "bring within the reach of young persons a science which no English writer has yet presented in an easy and familiar form."[52] Today's awareness of the importance of economic literacy in a free society has been implemented by the efforts of professional economists, educators, journalists, government officials, business leaders, and concerned organizations. A standing com-

---

*Sixteen editions of *Conversations on Political Economy* give testimony that Mrs. Marcet's book found contemporary favor.

†Popularly stated as "supply creates its own demand," Say's Law demonstrated that the income earned when men are employed provides enough purchasing power to absorb the product whereby overproduction and chronic unemployment are rendered impossible.

mittee on economic education was established by the American Economic Association in 1955. Since 1949 the Joint Council on Economic Education has worked through curriculum research, workshops, seminars, in-service education programs, and the preparation of materials for teachers and pupils from kindergarten to college to improve the quality of economic education. Teaching materials listed in the Joint Council's *Checklist* for September 1970 would seem to have been inspired by Jane Marcet's initial effort, to wit: *Learning Economics Through Children's Stories,* Bibliography for Grades K-3; *Teachers Guides to Economics* for Grades 1 to 8; *Goods, Services, and People,* An Economics Sequence for the Primary Grades; *Economic Themes in United States History.* The materials and treatment today—different, of course, from that of the dogmatic moralistic narratives employed by Jane Marcet and her immediate successors—aim to provide tools of analysis and an understanding of the structure and workings of the economy which will enable citizens to arrive at their own rational choices.

Mrs. Marcet made no claim for originality, but the purpose for which she wrote and the treatment she gave her subject matter were original. Her dialogues and stories introduced political economy to many who would otherwise have known nothing about it. Her work stimulated subsequent writers, launched economic education, and influenced economic thinking both in and beyond her time. From present perspective, we can believe that Mrs. Marcet's method of popularization helped to bridge the gap between the first scholarly treatises on political economy and the systematic textlike treatises which were soon to follow and which abound today. Mrs. Marcet's stories became the prototype for the work of two women, notable in economics, who were to follow.

NOTES

1. Quoted in William Letwin, *The Origins of Scientific Economics* (New York: Doubleday, 1964), p. 90.
2. R. K. Webb, *Harriet Martineau, A Radical Victorian* (New York: Columbia University Press, 1960), p. 102.

3. Jane Haldimand Marcet, *Conversations on Political Economy; in which the Elements of that Science are familiarly explained,* 5th ed. (London, 1824), Preface III.
4. "William Haldimand," *Dictionary of National Biography.*
5. Pierro Sraffa, ed., *Works of David Ricardo,* vol. 5, *Speeches and Evidence* (Cambridge, 1955), p. 353.
6. Ibid., vol. 10, *Biographical Miscellany,* p. 49.
7. Ibid., vol. 5, p. 352.
8. Ibid., vol. 10, p. 172.
9. Ralph M. Wardle, *Mary Wollstonecraft, A Critical Biography* (University of Kansas Press, 1951).
10. Mary Wollstonecraft, *A Vindication of the Rights of Woman,* Everyman's Library (New York: E. P. Dutton, 1929).
11. Wardle, op. cit., p. 168.
12. Wollstonecraft, op. cit., p. 174.
13. Ibid., p. 197.
14. Ibid., p. 186.
15. Ibid.
16. Letwin, *The Origins of Scientific Economics,* p. 96 ff.
17. There are twenty-six titles listed in the library of the British Museum, London.
18. Marcet, *Conversations on Political Economy,* op. cit., Preface III.
19. Ibid., Preface VI.
20. Ibid., p. 5.
21. Ibid., pp. 5-12, passim.
22. Ibid., p. 25.
23. Ibid., Preface IV.
24. Ibid., p. 173.
25. Ibid., p. 278.
26. Ibid., p. 188.
27. Ibid., p. 195.
28. Ibid., p. 200.
29. Ibid., p. 306.
30. Ibid., p. 176.
31. Ibid., p. 132.
32. Ibid., p. 168.
33. Webb, *Harriet Martineau,* pp. 106-107, and Webb, *The British Working Class Reader, 1790-1848* (London: George Allen and Unwin, 1955), passim.
34. *John Hopkins's Notions on Political Economy,* by the author of *Conversations on Chemistry, Political Economy, etc.* (Boston, 1833). Advertisement.
35. Ibid., p. 5.
36. Ibid., p. 25.
37. Ibid., p. 39.

38. Ibid., p. 155.
39. Marcet, *Conversations on Political Economy*, pp. 80-81.
40. Ibid., p. 94.
41. Jane Haldimand Marcet, *Rich and Poor* (Longman, Brown, Green and Longman 1851), Preface.
42. Ibid., p. 1.
43. Ibid., p. 13.
44. Ibid., p. 19.
45. Ibid., p. 23.
46. Marcet, *Conversations on Political Economy*, Preface V.
47. Sraffa, *Works of David Ricardo*, vol. 10, p. 172.
48. *Dictionary of National Biography*, vol. 12, pp. 1007-1008.
49. Ibid.
50. Ibid.
51. Marcet, *Conversations on Political Economy*, Preface IV.
52. Ibid., Preface III.

CHAPTER II

Harriet Martineau
(1802-1876)

> "Maggie, we've reached the top of the wave.
> There's not much more to be done. We're
> there!"
> —Thornton Wilder, *The Skin of Our Teeth*

Not all little English girls were as resistant to learning political economy as was Mrs. Marcet's Caroline. One young maiden in fact became interested in this subject on her own initiative before she was eleven, though like "poor Mr. Jourdain," she did not know that the subject of her interest was called political economy.

That little girl was Harriet Martineau. At an early age in her native Norwich, she read the "Globe" newspaper which, as she later wrote, ". . . without mentioning Political Economy . . . taught it and viewed public affairs in its light," helping her to "become a political economist without knowing it."[1] At age eleven she had displayed such unusual interest in economic topics that she was recognized by her brothers as an authority on the national debt. When she lost at games the family played at home, she would be given the forfeit "to make every person present understand the operation of the Sinking Fund."[2]

Harriet Martineau was the sixth child in a remarkable family of eight whose French Huguenot forebears had emigrated to England in 1686. Her father was a prosperous textile manufacturer in Norwich, where the family had a secure social position. Her mother was intelligent and ambitious for her children to have a good education. In young Harriet's time it was not considered proper for girls to be serious students; they were to learn only how to cook and to sew, and maybe something about the arts. But Harriet Martineau's early education consisted of reading, writing, arithmetic, and Latin taught by her older brothers and a sister, and instruction in Latin, French, and music under the guidance of tutors. She was encouraged to read history, biography, and literature aloud in the family circle. At the age of fifteen, she attended a school in Bristol for fifteen months and there, under the influence of the great Unitarian preacher and teacher, Lant Carpenter, she was influenced to read widely in religion and philosophy. It was in Bristol that she became aware of and accepted the philosophy of necessarianism which teaches that knowledge is supreme and individual exertion is a duty—a philosophical code that guided her throughout her life.

The Martineau business failed in the financial crisis of 1825-1826. Her father died in 1826, whereafter Harriet became completely dependent on her own resources. She began despite the fact that she had been afflicted with deafness from the age of fourteen, to earn a living for herself and her mother by needlework and by writing. Her first compositions were on religious subjects, and her first book, *Devotional Exercises,* had been published in 1823.

In 1827, she wrote a tract (one hundred and twenty-two pages) on the destruction of machinery by workers, a frequent form of social protest at the time. It was titled "The Rioters, or a tale of bad times." She said: "My Globe newspaper readings suggested to me the subject of Machine-breaking as a good one,—some recent outrages of that sort having taken place; but I had not the remotest idea that I was meditating writing on Political Economy, the very name of which was then either unknown to me or conveyed no meaning."[3] Another (one hundred and thirty-five pages) written at the same time, "The Turn Out, or Patience the best policy," dealt with the futility of strikes. These and other tracts which followed were published anonymously, her publisher paying the author a sovereign (one pound) apiece for them and selling the copies for a penny each.

It was in late 1827 that Harriet Martineau read Mrs. Marcet's *Conversations on Political Economy.* "I took up the book," she wrote later, "chiefly to see what Political Economy precisely was; and great was my surprise to find that I had been teaching it unawares, in my stories about Machinery and Wages. It struck me at once that the principles of the whole science might be advantageously conveyed in the same way,—not by being smothered up in a story, but by being exhibited in their natural workings in selected passages of social life."[4] Thus was conceived Harriet Martineau's *Illustrations of Political Economy* (1834), the inspiration for which, she readily acknowledged, "date[s] from my reading of Mrs. Marcet's *Conversations*. During the reading, groups of personages rose up from the pages, and a procession of action glided through its arguments, as afterwards from the pages of Adam Smith, and all the other Economists."[5]

Harriet Martineau chose the narrative form of exposition, then new to political economy,[6] because she was convinced it was the best form in which to teach the subject. She wrote: "This method of teaching Political Economy has never yet been tried, except in the instance of a short story or separate passage here and there. This is the method in which we propose to convey the leading truths of Political Economy, as soundly, as systematically, as clearly and faithfully, as the utmost painstaking and the strongest attachment to the subject will enable us to do. . . . We declare frankly that our object is to teach Political Economy, and that we have chosen this method not only because it is new, not only because it is entertaining, but because we think it the most faithful and the most complete."[7]

She deplored the dry obscurity of the systematic economics treatises then available, and observed: "They give us truths, and leave us to look about us, and go hither and thither in search of illustrations of those truths. . . . We cannot see why the truth and its application should not go together,—why an explanation of the principles which regulate society should not be made more clear and interesting at the same time by pictures of what those principles are actually doing in communities."[8]

While the time seemed propitious, it was not easy to find a sponsor for her project. She wrote to a succession of publishers, including the Society for the Diffusion of Useful Knowledge, which had indicated, when it was organized in 1826, that tracts on political economy would be among its publications. Each rejected her plan. She clashed with several over terms and title. She told how "they wanted to suppress the words Political Economy altogether: but I knew that science could not be smuggled in anonymously."[9] She persisted courageously, convinced of the importance of her undertaking, and stated her aim as follows: "If it concerns rulers that their measures should be wise, if it concerns the wealthy that their property should be secure, the middling classes that their industry should be rewarded, the poor that their hardships should be redressed, it concerns all that Political Economy should be understood."[10]

Ultimately Charles and William J. Fox reluctantly undertook publication, with no guarantee of recompense, because they had been counseled by the economist James Mill that Miss Martineau's plan "could not possibly succeed."[11] The stories were first published individually, and later the entire series was published in nine volumes, most of which contained three stories averaging about one hundred and thirty duodecimo pages each.

In an amazingly short interval after the appearance of the first number, *Life in the Wilds*—a Robinson Crusoe-type tale—it was evident that the project would be a success. The author, then age twenty-nine, later dated her release from financial worry with the publication on February 10, 1832, of this first number of the *Illustrations of Political Economy*. Reviews in all the daily and weekly papers were congratulatory. The Society for the Diffusion of Useful Knowledge then would have liked the whole series, and others bid for it at any price she cared to name, or made liberal offers, "the meanest of which I should have clutched at a few weeks before."[12] Within ten days from publication the first printing of two thousand copies was nearly exhausted and her publisher proposed a reissue of five thousand copies after any corrections she might wish to make. Ultimately ten thousand copies were sold—clearly a best seller, considering the date and the subject. Numerous editions appeared in both Great Britain and America.

Her original plan to have the stories appear quarterly was overruled by William Fox, who prevailed upon her to have them appear monthly for a period of two years. She reported: "The idea was overwhelming at first: and there were times when truly I was scared at other parts of the scheme than that. . . . I could never have even started my project but for my thorough, well-considered, steady conviction that the work was wanted,—was even craved by the popular mind."[13]

The stories were built loosely around James Mill's classical definition of political economy: Production, Exchange, Distribution, and Consumption of Wealth. But this outline was concealed under intriguing titles and chapter headings, intended to draw the reader into the tales from sheer curiosity. Even today some of the typically Victorian titles sound beguiling, and one expects anything but enlightenment on political economy.

Story titles in *Illustrations of Political Economy* are:

<table>
<tr><td>I.</td><td>Life in the Wilds</td></tr>
<tr><td>II.</td><td>The Hill and the Valley</td></tr>
<tr><td>III.</td><td>Brooke and Brooke Farm</td></tr>
<tr><td>IV.</td><td>Demarara</td></tr>
<tr><td>V.</td><td>Ella of Garveloch</td></tr>
<tr><td>VI.</td><td>Weal and Woe in Garveloch</td></tr>
<tr><td>VII.</td><td>A Manchester Strike</td></tr>
<tr><td>VIII.</td><td>Cousin Marshall</td></tr>
<tr><td>IX.</td><td>Ireland</td></tr>
<tr><td>X.</td><td>Homes Abroad</td></tr>
<tr><td>XI.</td><td>For Each and for All</td></tr>
<tr><td>XII.</td><td>French Wines and Politics</td></tr>
<tr><td>XIII.</td><td>The Charmed Sea</td></tr>
<tr><td>XIV.</td><td>Berkeley the Banker—Part I</td></tr>
<tr><td>XV.</td><td>Berkeley the Banker—Part II</td></tr>
<tr><td>XVI.</td><td>Messrs. Vanderput and Snoek</td></tr>
<tr><td>XVII.</td><td>The Loom and the Lugger—Part I</td></tr>
<tr><td>XVIII.</td><td>The Loom and the Lugger—Part II</td></tr>
<tr><td>XIX.</td><td>Sowers Not Reapers</td></tr>
<tr><td>XX.</td><td>Cinnamon and Pearls</td></tr>
<tr><td>XXI.</td><td>A Tale of the Tyne</td></tr>
<tr><td>XXII.</td><td>Briery Creek</td></tr>
<tr><td>XXIII.</td><td>The Three Ages</td></tr>
<tr><td>XXIV.</td><td>The Farrers of Budge-Row</td></tr>
<tr><td>XXV.</td><td>The Moral of Many Fables</td></tr>
</table>

Chapter headings are even more disarming. Some chosen at random are:

"Fasters and Feasters"
"A Mushroom City"

"Loyalty Preventives"
"Being Roman at Rome"
"Death-chamber Soothings"
"How to Entertain Strangers"

Miss Martineau made use of all the standard works on political economy then available,[14] some of whose authors she was later to know personally. Adam Smith's *The Wealth of Nations,* Thomas Robert Malthus' *An Essay on the Principle of Population,* and James Mill's *Elements of Political Economy* were her chief sources. But she made such clever use of other materials to round out the settings of her stories that it was said for example, in the case of "A Manchester Strike," that the Manchester operatives supposed the author "to have 'spent all her life in a cotton-mill.' "[15] The stories "Vanderput and Snoek" and "Feats on the Fiord" were thought to have been preceded by extended residence in Holland and Norway but she had never visited either country. Without the help of a secretary, she completed the twenty-five stories in the political economy series—each more than one hundred pages—to appear monthly over two years, a prodigious feat of self-discipline. In her *Autobiography* Miss Martineau revealed: "As to the actual writing,—I did it as I write letters, . . . never altering the expression as it came fresh from my brain. On an average I wrote twelve pages a day,—on large letter paper . . . the page containing thirty-three lines."[16]

The stories in *Illustrations* were followed immediately by five others entitled *Illustrations of Taxation.* Four others, entitled *Poor Laws and Paupers, Illustrated,* appeared simultaneously. Throughout this period subjects were continually being recommended to her by her readers—members of parliament, cabinet ministers, newspaper editors, factory owners and workers—but some of those subjects, she said, "had no more to do [with political economy] than geometry or the atomic theory."[17]

Favorite theses of each of the classical economists were reflected in her work. Her purpose, she declared, was "to write on subjects of universal concern as to inform some minds and stir up others."[18] She supported Adam Smith's doctrine of the harmony of interests wholeheartedly. The Malthusian principle of overpopulation as the basic cause of all social ills was stressed repeatedly. Ricardo's argument for free trade based on comparative advantage and Ricardo's wages-fund doctrine were developed persuasively. As with Mrs. Marcet, her acceptance of Say's Law of Markets is implicit throughout.

Some of the political economy tales vigorously challenged vested interests and monopoly privileges of the financial and manufacturing community, and pointed out social abuses in the existing order. Others of the stories demonstrated to working men the futility of striking and rioting, thereby giving support to the pre-Ricardian harmony-of-interest thesis between workers and capitalists, since "the interests of the two classes of producers, Labourers and Capitalists, are . . . the same; the prosperity of both depending on the accumulation of CAPITAL."[19] Here she clearly rejected the then popular Ricardian position that the two classes were in permanent conflict because a rise in wages would inevitably result in a decline in profits. Yet, by reason of her treatment of "a half-dozen fundamental topics" on which "she took a distinctly Ricardian stand à la James Mill" she is usually classed by scholars "as a disseminator of Ricardian economics."[20]

Most writers of the period, whether writing for children or adults, felt obliged to fulfill a serious purpose. Harriet Martineau was no exception. To make certain that her readers had not missed the economic message of the story, she presented as a conclusion a two- or three-page outline summary* of the economic principles she had treated in each story which "the reader could either read or as easily ignore."[21]

The twenty-fifth "story" in the *Illustrations* served the purpose of being a conclusion for the entire series. It is a systematic, text-like discourse of one hundred and forty-four pages titled *The Moral of Many Fables,* which summarized political economy according to the following outline:

Introduction

Part 1.   PRODUCTION: Large Farms; Slavery.

*For these she drew from James Mill's *Elements of Political Economy* for economic concepts and interpretations.

Here the principles of political economy, which in 1834 were widely thought to be complete as to definitions, laws, and practical application, were presented systematically. At the same time she acknowledged the philosophy to which she was devoted throughout her life, viz., the philosophy of necessarianism. Miss Martineau wrote: "What, then, is the moral of my fables? That we must mend our ways and be hopeful; or, be hopeful and mend our ways. Each of these comes of the other, and each is pointed out by past experience to be our duty, as it ought to be our pleasure. Enough has been said to prove that we must mend our ways: but I feel as if enough could never be said in the enforcement of hopefulness. . . . [Men] have made a vast approach towards being employed according to their capacities, and rewarded according to their works,—that is, towards participating in the most perfect conceivable condition of society. . . . The means and the end [for the good society is] THE EMPLOYMENT OF ALL POWERS AND ALL MATERIALS, THE NATURAL RECOMPENSE OF ALL ACTION, AND THE CONSEQUENT ACCOMPLISHMENT OF THE HAPPINESS OF THE GREATEST NUMBER, IF NOT OF ALL."[22]

The philosophy of necessarianism which Harriet Martineau embraced taught the need for the utmost exertion on the part of each individual to bring himself into line with the natural laws of the universe. The necessarian believed that for every result there is a cause, and the knowledge and use of these causes put the individual's fate in his own hands. Necessarianism presented a strong case for popular education. It was viewed as a moral sin for an individual to remain in ignorance. The necessarian believed that individuals could be so formed by education and by an actively diffused morality that the natural laws would operate to produce a happy, vigorous society. Hence, if people wished to improve their lot, if they wanted social reform, if they wanted the good society, they had to begin by informing themselves. Their interests, governed by the principles of political economy thus learned, would be properly reflected in government action. There is no doubt that for Harriet Martineau economics was a moral science, and education was the salvation of the good society.

Miss Martineau came to the philosophy of necessarianism via the writings of the psychologist David Hartley and his disciples Joseph Priestley and Lant Carpenter, the latter her teacher at Bristol in 1818. She testified to this influence when she wrote in her autobiography in 1855: "It was no wonder if Hartley became my idol when I was mistress of my own course of study. . . . I cannot at this hour look at the portrait of Hartley . . . without a strong revival of the old mood of earnest desire of self-discipline, and devotion to duty which I derived from [him] in my youth."[23]

In espousing the philosophy of necessarianism, she rejected perforce, the moral philosophy of sympathy (empathy), which Adam Smith had developed in his *Theory of Moral Sentiments* (1759) but had never fully incorporated in his economic doctrine. She also rejected the philosophy of Utilitarianism as expounded by David Hume, Jeremy Bentham, and James Mill, despite the fact that she quoted with approval the Utilitarian dictum: the greatest happiness of the greatest number.

Reading Harriet Martineau's synthetic fictionalized treatment of political economy today proves disappointing to the modern reader. Too often the author's style reflects her hasty, unrevised composition. For modern tastes, her stories provide neither entertainment nor enlightenment. The characters are stereotypes, not persons, the plots are mechanical, the style is humorless and ponderous, written at a time when verbiage reigned supreme. In spite of the pretense of narrative, the stories teach didactically an undigested dogma, and the modern reader may rightfully criticize and regret the author's economic naiveté, her unawareness of significant distinctions within the economic doctrine of the masters, and her incapacity or unwillingness to note the origins or to resolve the differences between the optimism of Smith and the pessimism of Ricardo.

Admittedly, by reason of the oversimplification of which both Harriet Martineau and Jane Marcet were guilty, they contributed, along with opinionmakers from all walks of life, as much to the subsequent confusion that beset economics as they contributed to its popularity and progress at the time. We are reminded that "New ideas are not likely to be welcome when everyone is already furnished with easy answers to difficult questions. Thus, by depriving Ricardo's critics of a receptive audience, the *Illustrations* played a significant role in holding back the reaction to Ricardian economics."[24]

But even as we deplore the synthetic fictionalized treatment she gave the subject, we cannot deny that in their day the political economy stories were a successful experiment in adult education. Not only did the stories sell well; they caused Miss Martineau to become almost overnight a recognized celebrity in social, political, and literary circles. Princess Victoria, as a young teen-ager, read her stories eagerly. Samuel Taylor Coleridge told Miss Martineau that he read her tales as they came out on the first of each month. By reason of these and her subsequent writings, Miss Martineau came to know many of the great and the near-great of her time, first as a resident in London after 1832, later in Tynemouth as an invalid, and still later as a householder at Ambleside in the Lake District, where she made her home after 1845.

Without false modesty Harriet Martineau acknowledged that she had successfully popularized the subject of political economy, but at no time did she claim originality as an economist. She aimed to overcome criticisms that political economy was dull and difficult, and sought to present it in a familiar, practical form, understandable to all. She considered dedicating her "slight elementary work" "to all whom it may concern." However, she recognized that this "would be the same thing as appealing to the total population of the empire" for "it concerns all that Political Economy should be understood."[25] Her own self-appraisal, written in

February 1834, appears in the preface to *The Moral of Many Fables:*

> It must be perfectly needless to explain what I owe to preceding writers on the science of which I have treated. Such an acknowledgment could only accompany a pretension of my own to have added something to the science—a pretension which I have never made. By dwelling, as I have been led to do, on their discoveries, I have become too much awakened to the glory to dream of sharing the honour. Great men must have their hewers of wood and drawers of water; and scientific discoverers must be followed by those who will popularize their discoveries. When the woodman finds it necessary to explain that the forest is not of his planting, I may begin to particularize my obligations to Smith and Malthus, and others of their high order.[26]

It is unjust to imply that one can appraise Harriet Martineau as a person or her entire career solely in terms of her political economy tales which were written in her early thirties. It was personal economic necessity and a keen journalistic sense of timing that drew her to write on political economy. She never returned to writing on economics thereafter. Seen in the perspective of a long life, the political economy tales occupied but a small corner of her life. Indeed later, writing in her autobiography, she deprecated the work: "After an interval of above twenty years, I have not courage to look at a single number,—convinced that I should be disgusted by bad taste and metaphysics in almost every page."[27] Doubtless she was also influenced by the belief, then current, that political economy had been fully developed so nothing remained to be added to its formal structure.

After the political economy stories, there followed a two-year interval between 1834 and 1836 of extended travel in America —a journey which then required a voyage of over thirty days by sailing ship. From this experience she produced two widely acclaimed books: *Society in America* and *Retrospect of Western Travel.* After a period from 1839 until 1844 of extreme malaise and invalidism, she built her home, The Knoll, at Ambleside, in the Lake District, and became the head of an active household.

She believed that no woman, married or single, could really be happy without a domestic life in which someone's health and happiness depended on her, and once, in a light moment, she described herself as "a good housemaid spoilt." Thereafter she continued, with energy and enthusiasm, as a sociological essayist, supporting national education and influencing thinking and legislation up to the time of her death at age seventy-four. Her prolific pen never rested, and much of lasting merit derives from her later works that were not on economics. Despite lifelong deafness and prolonged intervals of ill health, she was an indefatigable traveler, an astute observer, and a lucid, articulate reporter—the James Reston of her day. Her interests were far-flung and she wrote ceaselessly on a broad array of subjects—religion, philosophy, travel, sociology, politics—and in a variety of literary forms: essays, fiction, history, children's stories, letters, translations.

As with any astute journalist, the opinions she expressed were frequently ahead of her time. She supported actively the antislavery cause from the time she wrote her fourth political economy story, *Demarara,* in 1833, to the time when her efforts were no longer needed. She contributed more than ninety articles to an American abolitionist magazine over a two-year period, and it was said that she, more than any other person, kept "England straight in regard to America" on the issue of slavery.

Throughout life she had the welfare of the poor at heart, although she, no less than the classical economists of her time, was blind to exploitation when it became a source of national wealth. She advocated reform of the Poor Laws and believed strongly that the only way to improve the conditions of the workers was to improve their housing. In 1851 she was instrumental in the construction of thirteen "substantial grey stone cottages" for workers in the region where her own house was located. Yet, she was not a professional do-gooder; she condemned indiscriminate charity.

At a time when labor unions were opposed and workers could be prosecuted for striking, she took a firm stand for the right of labor unions to exist, although their power was to be limited to investigate, and to recommend remedies. In 1833 she wrote: "It is necessary for labourers to husband their strength by union, if it is ever to be balanced against the influence and wealth of capitalists."[28] Her break with the ideology of laissez faire on this subject was supported later by J. R. McCulloch who, writing in 1843, regarded prohibitions of workers' combinations as oppressive.[29] Yet she, as others of her time, supported the fallacious wages-fund doctrine which viewed capital primarily as an advance of wages made necessary by the fact that the worker had no property and could not support himself until the fruits of his labor materialized in a final product. The doctrine was used to oppose the right of workers to organize, and, as a theory of wages, was not discredited until 1870, and was not replaced until many years later by the marginal productivity theory.

Her self-assigned role was to "preserve and improve" the advantages of the social state, and her pen commanded respectful attention when she wrote in vigorous opposition to government interference in industry, or in support of direct taxation. She believed in the principles of democratic government and that social change must be undertaken within the democratic process. Yet she was frequently in dissent with the orthodoxies of both church and state, and she raised such searching questions on fundamental religious beliefs as to be condemned for her own unorthodoxy. She would be at home today with the current search for honesty and relevance in the modern climate of dissent and rebellion. On three different occasions she refused, as a matter of principle, a government pension in her own behalf.

Doctrinaire? Dogmatic? Eccentric? Yes, all of these. But also a person of deep conviction, of strong loyalties, of remarkable intelligence, and a joyous zest for living. Many biographies of Harriet Martineau have been written; they range from the sentimentally eulogistic to the uncharitably carping.* So complex and many-faceted a person provides substance for all. Although today she is largely ignored by economists, her *Illustrations of Political Economy* must stand as the first real attempt at adult economic educa-

---

*Fortunately a definitive and scholarly biography has been made available with the publication in 1960 of R. W. Webb's *Harriet Martineau, A Radical Victorian,* (New York: Columbia University Press, 1960).

tion. Scholars have described her later writings as "perceptive," "informed," "superb," "great." Supported by her necessarian philosophy which sustained her with purpose, self-discipline, and devotion to duty to the end, hers was the self-appointed role of the journalist-social scientist turned universal educator.

NOTES

1. *Harriet Martineau's Autobiography*, with Memorials by Maria Weston Chapman, 2 vols. (Boston, 1877), pp. 54-55.
2. Ibid., p. 54.
3. Ibid., p. 103.
4. Ibid., p. 105.
5. Ibid., p. 106.
6. For commentary on the popularity of the novel during the period, see R. K. Webb, *The British Working Class Reader 1790-1848* (London: George Allen and Unwin, 1955).
7. Harriet Martineau, *Illustrations of Political Economy*, 9 vols. (London: Charles Fox, 1834), Preface XII-XIII.
8. Ibid., Preface XII.
9. *Harriet Martineau's Autobiography*, vol. 1, p. 124.
10. Martineau, *Illustrations*, Preface XVI.
11. *Harriet Martineau's Autobiography*, vol. 1, p. 129.
12. Ibid., p. 136.
13. Ibid., p. 122.
14. Ibid., p. 147.
15. Ibid., p. 164.
16. Ibid., p. 148.
17. Ibid., p. 136.
18. Ibid., vol. 2, p. 166.
19. Martineau, *Illustrations*, vol. 1, *The Hill and the Valley*, p. 140.
20. Mark Blaug, *Ricardian Economics, A Historical Study* (New Haven: Yale University Press, 1958), p. 131.
21. Martineau, *Illustrations*, Preface XV.
22. Ibid., vol. 9, *The Moral of Many Fables*, pp. 140-144, passim.
23. *Harriet Martineau's Autobiography*, vol. 1, pp. 80-81.
24. Blaug, op. cit., p. 139.
25. *Illustrations*, vol. 1, Preface XV.
26. Ibid., vol. 9, *The Moral of Many Fables*, Preface VI.
27. *Harriet Martineau's Autobiography*, vol. 1, pp. 194-195.
28. *Illustrations*, vol. 7, *A Manchester Strike*.
29. *Harriet Martineau's Autobiography*, vol. 2, pp. 116-118.

CHAPTER III

Millicent
Garrett
Fawcett
(1847-1929)

> "We're not what you're all told and what
> you think we are; We're ourselves. And if
> any man can find one of us he'll learn why
> the whole universe was set in motion."
> —Thornton Wilder, *The Skin of Our Teeth*

Harriet Martineau's *Illustrations of Political Economy* reached
and influenced one who was to become more closely associated
with economic education than either of her predecessors, and
who was to continue the popularization of economics which they
had begun. Millicent Garrett, at the age of twenty, had married
Henry Fawcett (1833-1884), a professor of political economy at
Cambridge University and a member of Parliament, who was
fourteen years her senior. Their marriage was a happy union of
perfect interdependence. His wife was in entire sympathy with his
liberal views. He, in turn, gave support to her views on women's
suffrage and higher education for women. She was eyes and hands
to him in his blindness, aiding him in his studies and writings.
Their interests merged on the common grounds of economics,
education, and political reform. Several of their writings were
brought out under joint authorship. Mrs. Fawcett's place in the
development of economics and economic education is so closely associated with that of her husband that it can scarcely be viewed
separately. Together they are among the last nineteenth-century
spokesmen for pre-Marshallian economics in Great Britain.

In her long life Millicent Garrett Fawcett was to become
identified chiefly with politics and the Women's Suffrage Movement, but the influences that brought her into economics and into

this select company of the daughters of Adam Smith began before she met Henry Fawcett in 1865. She was the seventh child in a closely knit family of ten—six girls, four boys. Her father was a merchant and shipowner in Aldeburgh, in Suffolk, England. He was interested in politics, alert to civic responsibility, and active in the affairs of the community. A brief attendance for each of the sisters at a school at Blackheath stimulated their interest in literature, art, and music beyond the intellectual stimulation afforded by an exceptionally purposeful household.

Millicent had an example to emulate in her sister, Elizabeth— eleven years Millicent's senior—who struggled to secure a medical education and to be the first woman to enter the medical profession. Elizabeth achieved her goal in 1865, and her success was credited with opening the door of medical education for women in England.

Also in 1865, Millicent became aware of the writings of John Stuart Mill who was up for election to Parliament for the City of Westminster. She read and accepted Mill's philosophy and thought about the principles which ought to underlie public action. Mill had given strong approval to Women's Suffrage and his views brought the subject into the political world for the first time.

Thus the two subjects, politics and women's rights, were topics with which Millicent Garrett had been conversant before the age of eighteen when, at a party in May 1865, she met Henry Fawcett. He was attracted by the forthrightness of her comments on affairs of the day, and before the evening was over had fallen in love with her. He was then thirty-two years old, a professor of political economy at Cambridge University since 1863, a Member of Parliament from Brighton since 1864, and blind from a gunshot accident since 1858. They became engaged in October 1866, and were married in April 1867.

Thereafter they lived in Cambridge during the Fall term, and in London when Parliament was in session. Until 1871 she served as her husband's secretary, read and wrote for him, and they discussed matters of political interest and topics related to his Cambridge lectures, professional writings, and political speeches. Henry Fawcett was a resolute person who faced his blindness realistically, determined to cause his friends no trouble because of it. His considerable handicap had not deterred him from seeking a political career, nor of pursuing a profession in which he commanded high respect. He never asked for sympathy and desired to be treated as an equal. He loved to fish, to take long walks, and was, reportedly, a magnificent skater.

Three years after their marriage, Mrs. Fawcett published her *Political Economy for Beginners*. She stated in the preface to the first edition, which appeared in 1870: "When I was helping my husband to prepare a third edition of his *Manual of Political Economy,* it occurred to us both that a small book, explaining as briefly as possible the most important principles of the science, would be useful to beginners, and would perhaps be an assistance to those who are desirous of introducing the study of Political Economy into schools. It is mainly with the hope that a short and elementary book might help to make Political Economy a more popular study in boys' and girls' schools that the following pages have been written."[1] She also gave credit to Macmillan, her publisher, for the original idea of the book and for its format.

Political Economy for Beginners was an immediate success. It went through ten editions in 41 years, a pre-Samuelson record. Each edition was updated as to facts and illustrations, and new topics were introduced as they entered the popular scene. It reflected, as did Henry Fawcett's *Manual* (1863) on which it was based, the economic doctrine of John Stuart Mill, who was one of the Fawcetts' closest friends, and whose *Principles of Political Economy* (1848) was the foremost economic treatise of the time.

The tenth edition (1911) of *Political Economy for Beginners* presented the subject according to the following outline in two hundred and fifty-four compact pages.

Introduction

Section I.   THE PRODUCTION OF WEALTH
     Chapter I.   On Land
     Chapter II.   On Labour
     Chapter III. On Capital

Here is presented the essence of economics as it was understood prior to the appearance of Alfred Marshall's refinements. Repeated references are made to John Stuart Mill's *Principles of Political Economy*. The emphasis is on microeconomics, but without benefit of diagrams. Such macroeconomic topics as division of labor, population, cooperation, and taxation were treated without any integrating theme. Acceptance of Say's Law of Markets is implicit in the view that unemployment—a depression in trade— was only a temporary phenomenon and would always be cured by active competition. She wrote: "Where competition is active the effect of a local depression of Trade upon Wages is only temporary. When wages are below the average and trade is dull, an influence is exerted by these very circumstances to restore wages and profits to their normal condition. Manufacturers will not go on producing commodities at a comparative loss, and intelligent workmen will not go on labouring at an occupation in which they receive lower wages than they could obtain elsewhere. The supply of capital and labour engaged in the depressed trade is accordingly reduced; production is decreased, and the supply being diminished prices rise, and wages are restored to their former level."[2]

She carefully itemized the "radical defects" of socialism, not the least of which was removal of "the prudential restraints" on population growth, and she conceded: "The present system does not work so well as to be absolutely incapable of improvement; and though it may not be thought desirable that an alteration of existing economic arrangements should be made in the direction of socialism, we ought to be ready to admit that some improvement is necessary in a community in which a considerable proportion of the population are either paupers or are on the brink of pauperism."[3]

Although she was aware that the wages-fund doctrine had been challenged by scholars, and repudiated by John Stuart Mill, she continued to accept it, deeming it "not desirable in an elementary book to enter at length into the controversy on the wages-fund theory."[4] She stated repeatedly and emphatically: "A demand for commodities is not a demand for labour. The demand for labour is determined by the amount of capital directly devoted to the remuneration of labour: the demand for commodities simply determines in what direction labour shall be employed."[5]

She presented an extended discussion on the nature and functions of capital, after which she acknowledged: "The explanation of the functions of capital has probably presented some difficulty to the beginner,"[6] and again saw need to emphasize her position on the wages-fund theory with the following question at the end of the chapter: "Prove from the propositions enunciated in this chapter that the capitalist is the real benefactor of the wages-receiving classes, and not the spendthrift or the almsgiver."[7]

The resemblance between Mrs. Fawcett's systematic treatment of her subject and that of modern "outline" books makes the reader feel that some of the latter are lineal descendants of her publication. By means of concise, unqualified statements and homespun illustrations, she sought to promote knowledge of economic principles and their relation to the problems of everyday life. Questions and a "few little puzzles" appear at the end of each chapter, the latter intended to "serve as a vehicle for introducing a discussion."[8]

Some of the questions continue to be provocative, but others would undoubtedly evoke facetious answers from modern students. One can only imagine the kind of answers or discussion that would occur today if the following questions were posed:[9]

Is the labour of a boy writing Virgil for a punishment productive or unproductive?

What would become of undertakers if people left off dying?

Would it be good for trade if an explosion of gunpowder blew up the Houses of Parliament?

But other questions could be a starting point for a meaningful economic dialogue no less now than then:

Show by an illustration that, under certain circumstances, profits and wages can both be raised without increasing prices.[10]

Is usury wicked? Were the laws regulating the rate of interest any good?[11]

What is probably the reason why England has recognised the advantages of free trade before America?[12]

Ought any class of persons who avail themselves of the protection which a State affords enjoy immunity from taxation?[13]

In 1874 Mrs. Fawcett published four stories entitled *Tales in Political Economy*. She acknowledged her debt of authorship in the preface: "It is hoped that these little tales may be of some use to those who are trying to teach Political Economy. I cannot let them go to press without a word of apology to Miss Martineau for my plagiarism of the idea, which she made so popular thirty [*sic*] years ago, of hiding the powder, Political Economy, in the raspberry jam of a story."[14]

The individual story titles of the *Tales* indicate the vitality of the Robinson Crusoe theme, an ever-popular device after 1719, and one used by all the Classical economists with their fiction of the "economic man":

The Srimats
The Shipwrecked Sailors

Isle Pleasant
The Islanders' Experience of Foreign Trade

The Srimats were a group of self-sufficient islanders. The story demonstrated the advantages of free trade over protection of native industry. In addition, since "men will never pass laws involving loss to themselves,"[15] the story demonstrated the unwillingness of vested interests in a protected market to accept change.

"The Shipwrecked Sailors" demonstrated the benefits of division of labor and exchange, and the principles of competitive price. The law of diminishing returns could scarcely be reduced to more simple terms than is presented here in the homespun illustration found in the following: "If you took four boys to a cherry tree, and told them they might have as many cherries as they could gather in twenty minutes, they would get in that time many more than four other boys who were allowed to attack the tree afterwards for the same time and on the same conditions.[16] We have no way of knowing whether the author was inspired for this by the observation of Mrs. Marcet's "Mrs. B." that Maria Edgeworth's story "Cherry Orchard" might serve as a means of instructing children in political economy.

"Isle Pleasant" relates the difficulty of barter and the advantages and disadvantages of using coconuts for money.

The fourth story, "The Islanders' Experience of Foreign Trade," reveals how futile it is to "wait till your ship comes home" when that ship brings money, not goods, in exchange for export cargo—doubtless an attack on any vestigial mercantilists. Throughout her life Mrs. Fawcett was an ardent free trader and free enterpriser. She supported the principles of individualism brought out by these stories: individual thrift, individual initiative; she opposed all forms of government intervention, and she accepted the doctrine of the harmony of interests—that the real interests of labor and capital are identical.

Political Economy for Beginners and *Tales in Political Economy* are the only publications on political economy which Mrs. Fawcett wrote under her sole authorship. In the years that followed she wrote and published other books—fiction, history, biography—but none on the subject of political economy. However, in 1872, a volume titled *Essays and Lectures on Social and Political Subjects* was published under joint authorship with her husband. Each essay or lecture is identified by the initials of its author—six by H.F., eight by M.G.F. The following essays are credited to M.G.F.

The first two of these essays reflect Mrs. Fawcett's unqualified belief, shared by Henry Fawcett, in free enterprise. Essay III, written as a letter to the *Times,* December 1870, indicated her opposition to making elementary education free on the ground that to do so would have "demoralizing tendencies" by removing even more of the natural restraints on population than had already been removed by the Poor Law. "The poor laws raise the price of provisions and lower the real price of labour," she wrote, "by removing the natural restraints on population. . . . It is thus that poverty is perpetuated, and increased stores of suffering and misery are accumulated which will be borne by future generations."[17] She quoted John Stuart Mill and Herbert Spencer approvingly, and concluded that while compulsory education is necessary to a child's mental welfare, this is no ground for making education free. It is difficult for anyone today, reading an essay on this topic, to find that the subject could be discussed giving no consideration to the social benefits in a free society of universal free education, but this was not dealt with here.

Essay VI was published in *Macmillan's Magazine* in January 1872. In it Mrs. Fawcett decries the mounting size of the public debt and the mounting interest burden of the debt, citing especially conditions in France, Russia, Austria, and Italy. She expressed fear that commercial prosperity would suffer as capital funds were diverted from private production in order to invest in a public loan yielding interest at six percent. "This tendency to withdraw capital from industrial employment," she wrote, "is the first and most important of the dangers connected with the system of public loans."[18] A second criticism of public loans was that there was less assurance that the money raised by loans would be spent economically than was likely to follow for money raised by taxes. "Hence the limits of borrowing are about twenty times larger than the limits of taxation, and an amount that is monstrous as a tax, is (apparently) a very light burden as a loan. In consequence, borrowing is freed from the most powerful check that restrains taxation."[19] She cited as a third objection to the growing magnitude of national debt, the likely resort to protective tariffs to raise revenue. "In fact, it is openly avowed that the discussions on the Budget really turn on the old controversy between Free Trade and Protection; . . ."[20] She acknowledged that her moral objections to loans did not apply to capital improvement loans, nor to loans needful for national defense. On this she wrote, with words as thoughtful for 1972 as they were in 1872: "We often hear the present century spoken of as one of great enlightenment and civilization. If the extensive armaments of continental countries are necessary, in order to secure them from the rapacious designs of their neighbors, no boast should be made of the progress of civilization; if, on the contrary, these armaments are unnecessary, and the military expenditure is just so much money thrown away, then surely no boast should be made of enlightenment."[21]

Essays VIII and IX have a theme in common: the education of women. Together they provide as eloquent a statement for womens' liberation as any made for that cause in the 1970s. (Essay VIII appeared in the *Fortnightly Review,* November 1868; Essay IX was delivered as a lecture July 1871.) They contain Mrs. Fawcett's reflections on a report of a Schools' Inquiry Commission that had examined the state of Middle-Class Female education and had found it deficient. The commissioners had expressed dissatisfaction because of the "want of thoroughness and foundation" and the "slovenliness and showy superficiality"[22] of the teaching of girls. Too much time, they reported, was spent in acquiring "certain accomplishments of an ornamental, rather than of a intellectual kind"[23] while the cultivation of logical and critical faculties was found to be sadly neglected. The report credited this condition to the educational deficiencies of school governesses, the indifference of parents, and the lack of vocational opportunities for women. Parents, Mrs. Fawcett wrote, "give their sons a good education because it pays; they do not give their daughters a good education because it would not pay."[24]

"Why," she asked, "do not parents create an effectual demand for the improved education of women?"[25] Her answer, given often with biting sarcasm, stated that nearly all remunerative occupations were closed to women by law or custom; that it was generally thought that "money spent on educating a woman well is badly invested, and therefore it would be unwise to try to improve her education";[26] and that girls had been "practically excluded from the great educational endowments [scholarships] of the country."[27]

Observing that it is more needful "to train girls with the view of making them good and useful members of society, than to train them expressly for the duties of married life," Mrs. Fawcett continued, "the notion that it is right to educate a girl solely with the view of her marrying has its rise in the immorality of public opinion as regards the functions of womanhood. As long as the height of national prosperity is thought to be attained if the population doubles itself in twenty years; as long as women are considered useful members of society in proportion to the number of their children, so long will their intellectual and moral faculties be neglected. Their education will remain, as it is described by the commissioners, slovenly and superficial, when the highest duties of a wife and mother are practically considered to be to breed children and to keep house."[28]

The last four essays in this collection indicate by their titles that by 1872 Mrs. Fawcett was moving ever more deeply into the fields of political and social action. The two essays on women's suffrage (X and XI), filled with astute reasoning and cutting irony, demonstrate eloquently why she was to achieve fame as a women's liberationist.

With residence in Cambridge, Mrs. Fawcett was in the center of the movement for higher education of women in England. It was at a tea party in her drawing room in 1869 that discussion first took place for what was to become, in 1874, the first residence institution, Newnham Hall, for the higher education of women.* Millicent Fawcett served as a member of the Council of Newnham College for many years and was made very proud in 1890 when her daughter, Philippa Fawcett, graduated from Newnham with highest honors in mathematics.

Henry Fawcett died suddenly in November 1884. Alfred Marshall succeeded him in his post at Cambridge. From that time Mrs. Fawcett lived in London with her sister, Agnes Garrett, the only one of her nine sisters and brothers to survive her. Thereafter, it was natural for her to identify herself closely with the Women's Suffrage movement and she became the central figure in England in that long struggle. She had entered the movement in 1867 at a time when women were politically ineffective, and for more than fifty years she guided the movement skillfully. Success was achieved in England in 1918† It seems appropriate that Mrs. Fawcett should choose that greatest of all hymns to human freedom and loyalty—Beethoven's *Leonora Overture* No. III—to mark that triumph in a victory celebration and public program in March 1918.

---

*In that same early year, 1869, Mary Paley (later Mrs. Alfred Marshall) won a scholarship to Cambridge University and became one of the first of five women students to enter Cambridge in 1871. In 1874 Miss Paley took the Moral Sciences Tripos, which was the only examination at that time which included Political Eonomy. Mary Paley was invited in 1875 to be in residence at Newnham where she took over from Alfred Marshall "the task of lecturing on Economics to women students." Mary Paley and Alfred Marshall were married in 1877 and thereafter, for nearly half a century, her life was wholly merged in his. Theirs was an intellectual partnership not unlike the Fawcett's, based on profound dependence on his part, and deep devotion and admiration on hers. (See John Maynard Keynes, *Essays in Biography* [New York: W. W. Norton & Co., 1963], pp. 324-347.)

†Women's suffrage was approved in the United States in 1920 with the adoption of the nineteenth amendment to the Constitution.

The work in behalf of women's rights continues in both Great Britain and the United States. With political rights secured, attention is now directed towards achieving equal economic opportunities for women. It is of interest to note that on March 6, 1971, several thousand women demonstrated with a march from Hyde Park to Trafalgar Square in London for equal pay, equal job opportunities, and equal education with men, after which *The Economist* for April 3, 1971, wrote: "Yes, women do need liberation. . . . The female half of the population is nowhere near adequately represented in the political, intellectual or commercial life of Britain or any other country. . . . That they should still have to march to demand these is a very serious criticism of British society."[29] In the United States, the Civil Rights Act of 1964 forbids discrimination in employment on the basis of race and sex. There is little doubt that Millicent Garrett Fawcett, one of the earliest women's liberationists, would, if she were living today, applaud and aid this effort to lessen the waste of talent and the economic, social, and psychological cost which discrimination on the basis of sex, or on any other basis, entails.

Honors and recognition came to Mrs. Fawcett in her later years. In January 1899 an honorary degree "in recognition of her work for higher education of women" was awarded by St. Andrews University. In 1924 she was made a Dame Grand Cross of the Order of the British Empire, and was known thereafter as Dame Millicent. She died in 1929 at the age of eighty-two.

Although Mrs. Fawcett's influence on political economy was slight, nonetheless her contribution should never be ignored as we record the progress of economic education. As with Mrs. Marcet and Harriet Martineau, she made no doctrinal contribution to economic science. Yet, by the simplicity and clarity of her writing, she furthered a search, begun by Jane Marcet in 1816 and continuing in the present, for finding a way to make economics meaningful to the beginner and to the general reader, and this, she knew was important. And she contributed effectively to the women's rights movement which continues to challenge both the present and the future.

ADAM SMITH
(1723-1790)
Photograph by
Josiah Wedgwood & Sons Ltd.

HARRIET MARTINEAU
(1802-1876)
Portrait by
George Richmond, 1849
nal Portrait Gallery, London)

MILLICENT GARRETT FAWCETT
(1847-1929)
From a photograph
taken about 1892

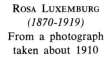

ROSA LUXEMBURG
(1870-1919)
From a photograph
taken about 1910

NOTES

1. Millicent Garrett Fawcett, *Political Economy for Beginners,* 10th ed. (London: Macmillan & Co., Ltd., 1911), Preface. Includes Preface to the First and other editions.
2. Ibid., p. 134.
3. Ibid., p. 45.
4. Ibid., p. 29, fn.
5. Ibid. p. 30.
6. Ibid., p. 39.
7. Ibid., p. 40.
8. Ibid., Preface to the Second Edition (1872).
9. Ibid., p. 25.
10. Ibid., p. 91.
11. Ibid., p. 156.
12. Ibid., p. 209.
13. Ibid., p. 251.
14. Millicent Garrett Fawcett, *Tales in Political Economy* (London: Macmillan & Co., Ltd., 1874), Preface.
15. Ibid., p. 10.
16. Ibid., p. 49.
17. Henry Fawcett and Millicent Garrett Fawcett, *Essays and Lectures on Social and Political Subjects,* (London: Macmillan & Co., Ltd., 1872), pp. 57, 63.
18. Ibid., p. 129.
19. Ibid., p. 131.
20. Ibid., p. 139.
21. Ibid., p. 135.
22. Ibid., p. 186.
23. Ibid., p. 192.
24. Ibid., p. 192.
25. Ibid., p. 215.
26. Ibid., p. 194.
27. Ibid., p. 194.
28. Ibid., pp. 200-201.
29. "The Underdeveloped Sex," in *The Economist Newspaper,* Ltd., London, April 3, 1971, p. 18.

CHAPTER IV

Rosa Luxemburg
(1870-1919)

> "There's no time to lose. Go. Push the animals along before you. Start a new world. Begin again."
> —Thornton Wilder, *The Skin of Our Teeth*

While the mainstream of traditional orthodox economics—as typified by the gentle, didactic writings of Jane Marcet, Harriet Martineau, and Millicent Fawcett—was flowing, seemingly smoothly, through the nineteenth century, a countertheme of social, political, and economic unrest was building up as reflected in the ideas and writings of utopian and revolutionary socialists, to reach a climax in mid-century in the writings of Karl Marx. Economics is a reactive science; economists, hearing the ideas of their predecessors and contemporaries, react to them with new ideas and insights. As the century advanced we find Rosa Luxemburg caught in the tempo of her times, providing vigorous leadership to this reaction on the left. Rosa Luxemburg was Adam Smith's most rebellious daughter.

The youngest of five children, Rosa Luxemburg was born into the family of a cultured and relatively prosperous Jewish merchant in the small Polish town of Zamosc near the Russian border. Her father, who had been educated in Germany, was in sympathy with but not politically active in the national-revolutionary movement. The family moved to Warsaw in 1873 where she received her early education. From her parents, who were conversant with Polish, Russian, and German thought and literature, Rosa Luxemburg acquired a cosmopolitan background. She graduated at sixteen at the head of her class from the girl's Gymnasium in Warsaw, but was denied the gold medal award for her achievement because of her "oppositional attitude toward the authorities."

During her school years her hatred mounted for the Russian authoritarianism of the schools. Her zeal for social justice drove her into joining the ranks of the Socialist Revolutionary movement. In the two years after leaving high school in 1887 she made her first acquaintance with the writings on scientific socialism, primarily the works of Marx and Engels. At nineteen, her political activities forced her to flee to Switzerland to escape arrest. Switzerland was at that time "the intellectual power station from which East European revolutionary movements were supplied."[1] In Switzerland she became acquainted with many Russian-Polish exiles and political refugees who were to influence and share her subsequent career and she was soon at the center of a political-intellectual ferment.

She earned her doctorate at the University of Zurich in 1897 in law and philosophy, after having first pursued courses in natural sciences and mathematics. Her doctoral thesis, "The Industrial Development of Poland," was her first contribution to economics. It achieved immediate commercial publication,* and was widely reviewed in Germany, Poland, and Russia. In it she analyzed the growth of Polish industry in the nineteenth century, demonstrating that Russian Poland had become so dependent on the Russian market that political demands for Polish independence were unrealistic. The economic evidence assembled and argument developed provided the basis for her continuing stand on this question. She used sources hitherto unknown or unavailable to Western students, a research approach that she successfully employed in her subsequent economic writings.

She moved to Germany in 1898 where she became a spokesman for Social Democracy and a leader of the extreme left wing of the international socialist movement. Her career, which advanced on two fronts, economic theorist and political activist, demonstrates that she was gifted with a brilliant mind, an intense,

---

*Die industrielle Entwicklung Polens. Inaugural Dissertation zur Erlangung der staatswissenschaftlichen Doctorwurde der hohen staatswissenschaftlichen Fakultät her Universität Zurich (The industrial development of Poland. Inaugural dissertation for the attainment of the doctorate in social sciences at the Higher Faculty of the University of Zürich), Leipsig, 1898.

questioning nature, great courage, and restless ambition. While her alert intelligence attracted her to several other areas of interest —painting, literature, poetry, anthropology, botany, geology, mathematics, any of which she might have pursued professionally because she studied each in depth and with enthusiasm—it was the two fields of economics and politics that claimed her lifelong attention, and where she made her mark.

Her political career, like that of Marx, implemented her economics, and economics was made to serve her political convictions. "Political power," she wrote, "is nothing but a vehicle for the economic process."[2] She became one of the acknowledged leaders of the left wing within the German working-class movement, participating actively from 1898 to the time of her death in 1919 in every undertaking that she believed would advance the revolution of the proletariat against the bourgeoisie. She was in the center of doctrinal and tactical disputes, a leader in the affairs of the Polish, Russian, and German Socialist parties, an organizer for mass activities, a principal speaker at Socialist meetings and congresses, and a featured writer for theoretical and popular journals. Always working in behalf of International Socialism, she battled against Polish nationalism, Eduard Bernstein's revisionism, and capitalism. Her intense political agitation for international socialism, her vitriolic polemics, her advocacy of the mass strike, and her uncompromising opposition to war made prosecution and jail a frequent and familiar experience after 1914. After a brief interval of freedom in late 1918 she was brutally murdered on January 16, 1919, in Berlin by a group of Prussian officers when she was being returned to prison. She died at the age of forty-eight, a foremost exponent and critical supporter of "democratic" Marxism.

In 1907 the German Social Democratic party had founded a party training school in Berlin, and Rosa Luxemburg was asked to lecture there on political economy. She became a brilliant interpreter of Marxism. During this period (1907-1912) she wrote her most notable economic work, *The Accumulation of Capital* (1913).

Capital accumulation is central to the subject of economic

growth, and as such has been studied by economists from Adam Smith to the present. Book II of *The Wealth of Nations* is titled "Of the Nature, Accumulation, and Employment of Stock." In it, Adam Smith wrote:

> Whatever a person saves from his revenue he adds to his capital, and either employs it himself in maintaining an additional number of productive hands, or enables some other person to do so, by lending it to him for an interest, that is, for a share of the profits. As the capital of an individual can be increased only by what he saves from his annual revenue or his annual gains, so the capital of a society, which is the same with that of all the individuals who compose it, can be increased only in the same manner.[3]

Capital accumulation was deemed desirable by Adam Smith because it contributed to industrial progress and stimulated population growth. The classical economists assumed that the rate at which capital would increase would vary according to profit, rising when the rate of profit rose and falling when the rate of profit fell.

When the emphasis of economists shifted from production to income distribution, Ricardo and his followers observed that profits and wages varied inversely with one another. Because of the assumed rigidity of the wage fund, which could be increased only as a result of saving by the capitalists, increases in either profits or wages could be achieved only at the expense of the other. The combined forces of increasing population and diminishing returns would mean that wages would be at subsistence level, and the future trend of profits would necessarily be downward, ultimately falling so low as to discourage all further accumulation, at which point society would have reached a stationary state. Ricardo wrote: "[The producers'] motive for accumulation will diminish with every diminution of profit, and will cease altogether when their profits are so low as not to afford them an adequate compensation for their trouble, and the risk which they must necessarily encounter in employing their capital productively."[4]

Karl Marx was nourished by the pessimism of Ricardian economics. If natural forces were to doom mankind to a grueling struggle for survival, was it not appropriate to abandon the class-ical philosophy of laissez faire and to reconstruct society? Marx accepted two weak points of Ricardo's analysis—the inadequate labor theory of value, and the characterization of property income as "unearned"—and adapted them to his own purpose. At the same time he reexamined the role of capital accumulation in an industrial society, devoting twelve chapters of *Capital* to the topic. His study led him to what he believed were the internal contra-dictions of capitalism: the Ricardian tendency to a falling rate of profit amid economic growth, large-scale industrial production leading to monopoly, technological unemployment, increasing class conflict, and increasingly severe industrial crises.

It is understandable, from the foregoing and with the empha-sis Marx gave to capital accumulation, why Rosa Luxemburg should study the subject. But Rosa Luxemburg found the treat-ment of the subject by both classical economists and Marx inade-quate or incomplete. In the thirty-two chapters (four hundred and seventy pages) of *The Accumulation of Capital*, she viewed capitalism in terms of its growth and sought to discover its gener-ative force by seeking solution to the problem of how social (aggregate) capital is annually renewed and augmented.

She developed her argument in three sections:

Section One: The Problem of Reproduction (9 chapters)
Section Two: Historical Exposition of the Problem (15 chapters)
Section Three: The Historical conditions of Accumulation (8 chapters)

She began by distinguishing between simple reproduction of capital where the entire output is consumed annually by workers and capitalists, and "enlarged reproduction", i.e., accumulation—the basis of economic growth. Although encumbered by Marxian terminology and assumptions, and made obtuse by mathematical models, Rosa Luxemburg gave a detailed explanation of simple reproduction of capital in a market economy. She also reviewed the treatment given the subject by many previous authorities both before and after Marx—seventeen in all—including the writings of several Polish and Russian writers little known to Western economists. She appraised these writings penetratingly, but often sarcastically and derisively, and always from a Marxian point of view. She provided, as had Marx, a painstakingly minute examination of the mechanisms of capitalist society. She revealed herself to be a more careful student of *The Wealth of Nations* than were many of Adam Smith's most ardent disciples, but she deplored the absence of social control in a free market and the lack of any plan to harmonize production and demand. "The first question a scientific examination of the laws of reproduction has to consider," she wrote, is "whether it is even possible to deduce anything like total reproduction from the disorderly jumble of individual capitals in constant motion, changing from moment to moment according to uncontrollable and incalculable laws, partly running a parallel course, and partly intersecting and cancelling each other out."[5]

Anticipating modern aggregative economics, she asked: "Can one actually talk of total social capital of society as an entity, and if so, what is the real meaning of the concept?"[6] She gave commendation to the Physiocrat, Francois Quesnay, because, in his *Tableau Économique* (1758) ("so intricate that no one before Marx could understand it") he "took it for granted that total capital exists as a real and active entity,"[7] while Adam Smith and Ricardo had been "doubtful, undecided and vacillating about this question."[8] "Indeed," she wrote, "almost every scientific economist up to the time of Marx concluded that there is no social capital."[9]

Yet she magnanimously acknowledged Adam Smith's discernment of "fundamental categories with regard to the reproduction and movement of circulating social capital. Fixed and circulating capital, private and social capital, private and social revenue, means of production and consumer goods, are marked out as comprehensive categories, and their real, objective interrelation is partly indicated and partly drowned in the subjective and theoretical contradictions of Smith's analysis."[10] With still further approval of Smith, she observed: "we may already perceive new connections within the social process of reproduction, understood by Smith in a deeper, more modern and vital way than was within

Quesnay's grasp, . . ."[11] whose "exposition, though showing flashes of genius, remains deficient and primitive."[12]

As she moved from a model of "simple reproduction" where the entire output annually is consumed by workers and capitalists, to one of "enlarged reproduction" i.e., accumulation, she found the treatments of all previous writers deficient in their search for a satisfactory explanation of accumulation. Their explanations, she observed, either interpreted only simple reproduction, thereby "refraining from accumulation," or explained accumulation in terms of cyclical phemonena which required stabilization policies, thereby "renouncing accumulation altogether."[13] After thorough examination she brusquely dismissed all previous explanations as useless and "confused" (Smith), "obviously absurd" (McCulloch), "trite" (Say), "regrettably clumsy" (Sismondi), "completely muddled" (Vorontsov), or "arrant nonsense" (Rodbertus).

Repeatedly she asked, without finding an answer in the writings on accumulation by her predecessors: "who are the buyers and consumers of the surplus product that comes into being if the capitalists produce more goods than are needed for their own and their workers' consumption; if, that is to say, they capitalize part of their surplus value and use it to expand production, to increase their capital?"[14] In short, she was asking: Why do capitalists invest? Condemning Say's classical "dogma" derisively, she wrote: "If society annually consumes its own total product completely, social reproduction without any means of production whatever must become an annual repetition of the Miracle of the Creation."[15]

Instead of the classical goals of production and profits, Rosa Luxemburg believed the prime motives of economic action to be consumption and income. She thus concluded "that only a socialist can really solve the problems of the reproduction of capital,"[16] but after an exhaustive and penetrating analysis of Marx's treatment of the question of accumulation, she was forced to admit, regretfully and apologetically, that "in the end Marx hardly touched upon it" because "polemics against [Adam Smith's theory of value] dominated Marx's analysis of the reproductive process."[17] She observed: "The analysis of the reproductive process, and the second volume of *Capital* finally comes to a close without having provided the long sought-for solution to our difficulty."[18] "Marx's diagram of enlarged reproduction," she wrote, "cannot explain the actual and historical process of accumulation. And why? Because of the very premises of the diagram. The diagram sets out to describe the accumulative process on the assumption that the capitalists and workers are the sole agents of capitalist consumption."[19] And again, she stated: Marx "could not supply immediately a finished solution either, partly because he was then preoccupied as we have shown, with denouncing the analysis of Adam Smith and thus rather lost sight of the main problem."[20]

It was Marx's contention that production and the acquisition of surplus value, i.e., profit, are the driving forces behind capitalism. Accumulation, for him, occurred as a result of capitalist employers using funds derived from surplus value to hire labor, thereby producing more surplus value, hiring additional labor, and so on ad infinitum, continually producing additional quantities of surplus value. From this, Marx proceeded to demonstrate the phenomena of the declining rate of profits and the recurrent crises afflicting an industrial economy—his contradictions of capitalism —whereby capitalism pursues a course destined for self-destruction. Marx viewed expansion as a "coercive law," and competition as the force that causes all enterprises to expand, thus causing capitalists to become "fanatical supporters of an expansion of production for production's sake."[21] Marx's explanation of capital accumulation is logical by reason of the fallacy of composition: First each capitalist tries to get ahead of others, later others are forced to keep up. But Rosa Luxemburg dismissed this thesis summarily. She wrote: "Competition, however wide we may make the concept, obviously cannot create values, nor can it create capitals which are not themselves the result of the reproductive process."[22]

Refusing to be sidetracked by the problem of crises, and with greater discernment than Marx, Rosa Luxemburg recognized the market as the force that generated enlarged reproduction. In her analysis of the operation of the free market she had observed that the production of the individual private producer "is determined entirely by the effective demand."[23] Turning to the reproduction of social capital, she wrote: "Now, however, the question arises whether the assumptions which were decisive in the case of individual capital, are also legitimate for the consideration of aggregate capital."[24] Here, she found that Marx, though working from different premises and ultimately diverted to different ends, had unknowingly supplied the answer. Marx had written: *"The conditions for the accumulation of capital are precisely those which rule its original production and reproducton in general. . . .* Accumulation of new capital can only proceed therefore under the same conditions under which already existing capital is reproduced."[25]

Thus taking her cue from Marx, Rosa Luxemburg searched for a social counterpart of the effective demand that served to generate individual production in the free market, and observed, for capitalist accumulation to be successful, "It requires as its prime condition . . . that there should be strata of buyers outside capitalist society."[26] "The accumulation of capital," she wrote, "as an historical process, depends in every respect upon non-capitalist social strata and forms of social organization."[27] In other words, capital accumulation depends on an increase in aggregate demand, and with this awareness the stage was set for Rosa Luxemburg's theory of imperialism, which she proceeded to develop in the final one hundred pages of her treatise.

Rosa Luxemburg arrived at her thesis of imperialism through deductive reasoning, but she proceeded to demonstrate it inductively by drawing from many other writings, and by recounting numerous historical experiences to illustrate the process of accumulation. By citing the economic history of British India, French Algeria, Egypt, the American West, Asiatic Turkey, and other economies, she demonstrated the importance of international trade and loans, protective tariffs, colonial exploitation, burdensome taxation, militarism and wars, as devices that had been used to advance the reach of European capitalism. "The general result of the struggle between capitalism and simple commodity production is this:" she wrote, "after substituting commodity economy [peasant economy] for natural economy, ["represented by the natives' primitive organizations"] capital takes the place of simple commodity economy. Non-capitalist organizations provide a fertile soil for capitalism; more strictly: capital feeds on the ruins of such organisations, and although this non-capitalist *milieu* is indispensable for accumulation, the latter proceeds at the cost of this medium nevertheless, by eating it up. Historically, the accumulation of capital is a kind of metabolism between capitalist economy and those pre-capitalist methods of production without which it cannot go on and which, in this light, it corrodes and assimilates. Thus capital cannot accumulate without the aid of non-capitalist organisations, nor, on the other hand, can it tolerate their continued existence side by side with itself. Only the continuous and progressive disintegration of non-capitalist organisations makes accumulation of capital possible."[28]

There is little doubt that Rosa Luxemburg's historical illustrations support adequately her theory of accumulation. The conditions which she described are not abstract conceptualizations; they are real objective phenomena, and as such, they are indisputable. But the question remains whether or not her abstract theoretical concepts and the real historical phenomena she describes can be causally linked to each other. Are these historical conditions the unavoidable consequence of accumulation under capitalism, or are they merely opportune manifestations of some specific social phenomenon? Couldn't an increase in aggregate demand come from an increase in population or per capita income? Also, how can capital accumulation proceed during the early stages of capitalism, before imperialism? In short, is economic imperialism the only path which history may follow? Rosa Luxemburg provides no answer to these questions.

But a still more fundamental question remains: Is it possible for capitalism to thrive in a closed economy? Rosa Luxemburg's answer to this question was a Marxist's resounding no, because "international trade is a prime necessity for the historical existence of capitalism"[29] and "real life has never known a self-sufficient capitalist society under the exclusive domination of the capitalist mode of production."[30] "Capitalism," she wrote, "needs non-capitalist social strata as a market for its surplus value, as a source of supply for its means of production and as a reservoir of labour power for its wage system."[31] "It is invariably accompanied by a growing militarism,"[32] which becomes "in itself a province of accumulation."[33] "Enlarged reproduction, i.e. accumulation," she stated emphatically, "is possible only if new districts with a non-capitalist civilisation, extending over large areas, appear on the scene and augment the number of consumers."[34]

With this analysis, she had arrived at a point where she could make her peace with Marx and return to the fold of Marxism orthodoxy. She too had reached, but by a different route, his conclusion that capitalism carries the seeds of its own destruction, and that socialism must eventually prevail. "Capitalism," she wrote to conclude her treatise, "is the first mode of economy with the weapon of propaganda, a mode which tends to engulf the entire globe and to stamp out all other economies tolerating no rival at its side. Yet at the same time it is also the first mode of economy which is unable to exist by itself, which needs other economic systems as a medium and soil. Although it strives to become universal, and, indeed, on account of this its tendency, it must break down—because it is immanently incapable of becoming a universal form of production. In its living history it is a contradiction in itself, and its movement of accumulation provides a solution to the conflict and aggravates it at the same time. At a certain stage of development there will be no other way out than the application of socialist principles. The aim of socialism is not accumulation but the satisfaction of toiling humanity's wants by developing the productive forces of the entire globe. And so we find that socialism is by its very nature an harmonious and universal system of economy."[35]

It is a heady, rewarding, but demanding experience for the modern student of economic thought to read *The Accumulation of Capital*. The author successfully communicates her own enthusiasms and her sense of urgency. The argument underlines today's struggle of ideologies. The bias is obvious. One is impressed, not only by the thoroughness of her critical reading of classical economics—especially *The Wealth of Nations*—but also with her temerity to criticize Marx, while never failing to acknowledge him as her master. Her analysis is not a theory of socialism, but a critique, as was Marx's, of capitalist economic development. As such, it confirmed her commitment to revolutionary socialism and underscored all her political activities.

Rosa Luxemburg was not the first economist to arrive at the subject of imperialism after making a critical study of classical economics and the profit system. One of the most famous was John A. Hobson (1858-1940), a prolific writer on economics and a British contemporary of Rosa Luxemburg. He was a dissenter, a self-styled economic heretic, who published a book titled *Imperialism** (1902) a decade before *The Accumulation of Capital* was to appear. Hobson's work provided detailed treatment of the economic origins of imperialism (seven chapters) and the political theory and practice of imperialism (seven chapters), while Rosa Luxemburg ignored its political and historical development as a condition indigenous to society and concentrated upon its effects on class relations. There is no way of knowing whether Rosa Luxemburg was aware of Hobson's work on this subject—she makes no reference to it, although she does mention him briefly in her appraisal of the inadequacy of the views of other writers on the question of social reproduction. Although they had traveled different routes, each arrived at the conclusion that imperialism, a consequence of capitalist growth, would lead inevitably to international rivalries, to militarism, and to war.

Lenin's pamphlet "Imperialism as the highest stage of Capitalism" was to follow *The Accumulation of Capital* by three years (1917). He insisted that advanced capitalism is inherently imperialistic and his criticism of Rosa Luxemburg's treatment of the subject for its lack of specific political content continued the disputes that had rankled between these two revolutionary socialists since 1903. Their differences over certain fundamental Marxist problems included the question of national self-determination, organizational questions and the role of party discipline, the crea-

---

*John A. Hobson, *Imperialism, A Study* (London: George Allen and Unwin, Ltd., 1902).

tive function produced by developing class consciousness and trade unionism, and the interpretation of Marx's doctrine of alienation of the proletariat from society. Rosa Luxemburg opposed Lenin's narrow authoritarian centralism while she espoused extension of democracy and freedom to the widest possible number of human beings. In all their controversies she viewed the forest, while Lenin saw the trees. Theirs was an illustration of the neverending contest between the long-run and the short-run; between the whole and the parts; between the overall view of the social philosopher and the segmented view of the social mechanic; between the generalist and the specialist. Both views are necessary if social understanding is to be complete. The differences between Rosa Luxemburg and Lenin were fundamental and prolonged, and never fully resolved. After her death, when she was no longer a threat to his leadership, Lenin detailed her doctrinal errors and ordered her works to be collected and published in their entirety.

Rosa Luxemburg's earliest concern with imperialism has been traced back to 1900[36] when she criticized the party's tolerance of German participation in the Chinese war. The subject became her central preoccupation after 1911. The subtitle to *The Accumulation of Capital,* "A Contribution to the economic clarification of imperialism," indicates her purpose had been to discover the cause of imperialism and its inevitability. Imperialism was the culmination—the *ne plus ultra*—of her economic analysis, as it became the focus of her political concerns. She provided no specific recommendations for challenging imperialism, nor did she develop a formula for organizing the postrevolutionary state. She stated her philosophy about it in 1915 as follows: "Imperialism as the last phase of the political world power of capitalism is the common enemy of the working classes of all countries, but it shares the same fate as previous phases of capitalism in that its own development increases the strength of its enemy *pro rata*. . . . Against imperialism the worker's class struggle must be intensified in peace as in war. This struggle is . . . both the proletariat's struggle for political power as well as the final confrontation between Socialism and capitalism."[37] This statement is number nine among the twelve declarations and six propositions adopted as a program for a party conference which Rosa Luxemburg had evolved and smuggled out of prison in December 1915.

New studies on imperialism continue to appear.[38] It is a lively modern topic, and while there is little agreement as to its depth or dimensions, there is universal agreement that it should be condemned.

With the exception of her doctoral thesis, *The Accumulation of Capital* is alone among Rosa Luxemburg's writings published during her lifetime to deal predominantly with economics. Originally published in 1913, it has reappeared in numerous editions in German and English, and in 1951, in an edition by the Yale University Press, with an introduction by Joan Robinson. After she had analyzed the successive Marxian models by means of which Rosa Luxemburg had developed her thesis, Professor Robinson rephrased the problem of accumulation in modern terms. The problem Rosa Luxemburg explored, she states, is the inducement to invest and "Investment can take place in an ever-accumulating stock of capital only if the capitalists are assured of an ever-expanding market for the goods which the capital will produce."[39] Professor Robinson recognized that Rosa Luxemburg had provided a theory of the dynamic development of capitalism and, in doing so, was on the threshold of a theory of investment, but Professor Robinson concluded: "her affinity seems to be with Hobson rather than Keynes."[40] By advancing imperialism as "her central thesis—that it is the invasion of primitive economies by capitalism which keeps the system alive,"[41] she left to John Maynard Keynes and others the development of the modern theory of investment.

Two other books by Rosa Luxemburg dealing with economics appeared posthumously. Neither is available in English. *Die Akkumulation des Kapitals oder was die Epigonen aus der Marxschen Theorie gemacht haben. Eine Antikritik* (The Accumulation of Capital or what the "authorities" have done with Marxist theory. An anti-critique) appeared in 1921. This is an answer to her critics of *The Accumulation of Capital* and was written in prison during World War I. It provides a simplified commentary designed to clear up some widespread misunderstandings, spear-headed by Lenin, to which *The Accumulation of Capital* had given rise. *Einfuhrung in die Nationalokonomie.* Hrsg. von Paul Levi (Introduction to political economy. Edited by Paul Levi), Berlin 1925, is a collection of her lectures delivered at the party training school in Berlin. It too, was completed in prison during World War I although she had worked on it from 1908 to 1911 before beginning work on *The Accumulation of Capital.* Apart from these writings, Rosa Luxemburg's economics was so inter-woven with her political activity as to make the two inseparable.

After the appearance in 1899 of Eduard Bernstein's work on revisionism, in which he argued for a modification of the Marxist dialectic, Rosa Luxemburg plunged headlong into the controversy as a defender of Marxian orthodoxy. Bernstein, believing that capitalism had a far greater potential for survival than Marx had realized, emphasized the moral content of socialism, with its capacity for redistributing income and opportunity. He advocated reform by means of continuing pressure by trade unions and cooperatives of producers and consumers, on and within the exist-ing system, instead of violent revolution. Rosa Luxemburg wrote a series of articles against revisionism which were issued together in 1899 under the title *Social Reform or Revolution* (a second edition appeared in 1907). This was "Rosa Luxemburg's most important contribution to the revisionist debate and the first of the great works of Marxist analysis on which her reputation rests."[42] In it she emphasized the need always to defend estab-lished orthodoxy against unwarranted innovations and she de-stroyed each of Bernstein's assumptions about the nature of capi-talism and the role of social democracy. "This detailed critique of Bernstein is still part of the standard tradition of Marxism up to the present day and can be found in every textbook on Marx-ism."[43] At the same time she condemned, with bitter contempt and invective, the German social scientists—Sombart, Schmoller, Roscher, Böhm-Bawerk for their advocacy of class collabora-tion and social harmony.

But merely to refute revision was, in her opinion, to main-tain the *status quo,* and for Rosa Luxemburg this was not enough.

After 1907 she developed her radical doctrine of the mass strike —a political weapon which, she conceived, should begin as a large-scale withdrawal of labor designed to upset the stability of the economy and serve as a prelude to a revolutionary struggle. The mass strike—not to be confused with the wage strike which had for its purpose the negotiation of better working conditions along with being a deliberate tool to sharpen class antagonisms to hasten the revolution—was essentially a process of interaction between political and economic activity.

After her death both Communists and Socialists claimed the authority of Rosa Luxemburg for their point of view—the former because of her advocacy of revolution, the latter because she had a deep feeling for democracy. She herself saw no conflict between the two because she viewed social revolution as a long-term—not short-term—transformation (the term "revolution" is always ambiguous), and she had an unswerving faith in the verdict of the majority of the people. She died, ever loyal to her Marxist orthodoxy, before an overt choice between these two "isms" had to be made. One can only guess where her allegiance would lie today in the contest between the Soviet Union and Communist China when the latter declares in a party program, adopted in April 1969, that "Mao Tse-tung thought is Marxism-Leninism of the era in which imperialism is heading for total collapse and socialism is advancing to worldwide victory."[44]

NOTES

1. J. P. Nettl, *Rosa Luxemburg,* 2 vols. (London: Oxford University Press, 1966), p. 45.
2. Rosa Luxemburg, *The Accumulation of Capital* (New Haven: Yale University Press, 1951), p. 452.
3. Adam Smith, *An Inquiry into the Nature and Causes of The Wealth of Nations* (New York: The Modern Library, 1937), p. 321.
4. David Ricardo, *On the Principles of Political Economy and Taxation,* 2d ed. (London: John Murray, 1819), p. 127.
5. Luxemburg, op. cit., p. 49.
6. Ibid., p. 49.

7. Ibid., p. 49.
8. Ibid., p. 54.
9. Ibid., p. 54.
10. Ibid., p. 61.
11. Ibid., p. 62.
12. Ibid., p. 50.
13. Ibid., p. 268.
14. Ibid., p. 206.
15. Ibid., p. 63.
16. Ibid., p. 106.
17. Ibid., p. 169.
18. Ibid., p. 154.
19. Ibid., p. 348.
20. Ibid., p. 351.
21. Ibid., p. 335.
22. Ibid., p. 342.
23. Ibid., p. 39.
24. Ibid., p. 349.
25. Ibid., p. 350.
26. Ibid., p. 351.
27. Ibid., p. 366.
28. Ibid., p. 416.
29. Ibid., p. 359.
30. Ibid., p. 348.
31. Ibid., p. 368.
32. Ibid., p. 371.
33. Ibid., p. 454.
34. Ibid., p. 429.
35. Ibid., p. 467.
36. Nettl, *Rosa Luxemburg.* abridged ed. (London: Oxford University Press, 1969), p. 161.
37. Nettl, op. cit., 1966 ed., p. 641.
38. For example see George Lichtheim, *Imperialism* (New York: Praeger Publishers, 1971) and Felix Greene, *The Enemy,* What Every American Should Know About Imperialism (New York: Random House, 1971).
39. Luxemburg, op. cit., p. 21.
40. Ibid., p. 21.
41. Ibid., p. 26.
42. Nettl, *Rosa Luxemburg,* abridged ed., p. 90.
43. Ibid., p. 133.
44. Quoted in a dispatch by Seymour Topping, *The New York Times,* June 28, 1971, p. 10.

CHAPTER V

Beatrice Potter Webb
(1858-1943)

"The whole world's at sixes and sevens, and why the house hasn't fallen down about our ears long ago is a miracle to me."
—Thornton Wilder, *The Skin of Our Teeth*

Adam Smith's fifth daughter, Beatrice Webb, was a one-woman embodiment of the Hegelian dialectic.* Both her personal life and her economic contributions illustrate Hegelian synthesis. In her personal life she combined harmoniously a satisfying career and a happy marriage at a time when for women career and marriage were thought incompatible; in her professional life she rejected both classical economic thought (the thesis) and Marxian economics (the antithesis) as she formulated her own philosophical synthesis of democratic collectivism for social organization. English Socialism, implemented by the Labour party after World War II, is greatly indebted to her for her ideas.

In order to appreciate fully the contributions of Beatrice Webb to economics and to society, it is necessary to examine some of the major social themes of her lifetime. To understand her, we must also understand the positions held, on the one hand, by the capitalist-individualists who were the practical beneficiar-

---

*The German philosopher Georg Wilhelm Friedrich Hegel (1770-1831) had set forth the theory that from a thesis that is confronted with a challenging antithesis, history is forever formulating a reconciling synthesis as it moves into new areas of social thought and action. He has been appraised by scholars as "possibly the most stupendous of all nineteenth century thinkers." R. R. Palmer and Joel Colton, *A History of the Modern World,* p. 439.

ies of the laissez-faire classicists (the social class from which she derived), and, on the other hand, by the revolutionary and constitutional socialists, from Karl Marx to the Fabians.

The Industrial Revolution, beginning in the late eighteenth century and continuing through the nineteenth century, had caused economic, social, and political changes throughout all levels of English society. England had become the most powerful nation in the world. Her burgeoning industrialism was accompanied by the growth of large urban centers that were ill equipped to provide for the multitudes who came to them from the country. Poverty and disease, made worse by overcrowding, became painfully visible in the urban areas. In the words of Beatrice Webb, written at a time when she was studying the roots of some social institutions, we read: "Mobs of starving factory hands paraded the manufacturing towns; secret societies honeycombed with sedition and conspiracy sprang up with amazing rapidity among the better paid artisans."[1] While economic and social changes were occurring, a parallel political change took place. Political power was transferred from the rural aristocracy to the middle class and to the capitalist-entrepreneurs. A major result of the Industrial Revolution was a pyramiding of material wealth which, in a period of unprecedented national prosperity, left thirty percent of the inhabitants of London in destitution and chronic poverty.[2]

The capitalists—merchants and maufacturers—were understandably proud of their accomplishments. They pointed to the rapidly increasing production of goods, to the opportunities for personal profits, and to the accumulation of property as proofs that the laissez-faire system was successful. They found satisfaction in the fact that England, by becoming the workshop of the world, had become prosperous. But the capitalist's success was self-centered. He believed that society progressed by reason of his personal accomplishments. In the words of Beatrice Webb: "The greed of gain, the passion for wealth, excited by social ambition and by an enjoyment of luxury hitherto unknown, overpowered the thoughts and feelings of middle and upper class Englishmen."[3] Their success obscured their vision of events and conditions by which they, personally, were not affected, viz., unemployment, poverty, malnutrition—ills that afflicted a disturbingly large segment of the population.

Furthermore, a rather libertarian interpretation of the Smith-Malthus-Ricardo doctrine of laissez faire provided the rationalization to many capitalists to remain complacent in the face of society's ills. In short, they believed that poverty was a man's own fault and should be treated as a crime, with every man left to suffer the consequences of his own action. Three broad themes were constantly reiterated: (1) people should work harder; (2) only the lazy and incompetent were poor; and (3) persistent effort on the part of the indigent would yield a better civilization. These ideas were dominant in the economic philosophy of Victorian England.

Concentration upon social ills is one-sided. England was the first country in modern times to experience a quickening of social consciousness, and by the mid-nineteenth century many meaningful reforms were under way. A foremost modern authority on the period records: "A careful reading of the reports [of Royal Commissions] would, indeed, lead to the conclusion that much that was wrong was the result of laws, customs, habits, and forms of organization that belonged to earlier periods and were rapidly becoming obsolete."[4] Among the social critics and reformers three groups emerged: the utopian socialists, typified by Robert Owen in the 1820s; the evolutionary socialists, and the revolutionary socialists. They were united in one belief that the meaning of progress was more than the accumulation of wealth by a relatively few; instead they defined progress as a more equitable distribution of the fruits of economic growth. Karl Marx spearheaded the opposition in the 1850s and 1860s. He believed that the wealth that capitalism was transferring to the bourgeoisie (the middle class) and the capitalists belonged rightfully to the proletariat (the workers). Marx felt that the capitalistic economic system had to be overthrown through revolution in order to create a classless society where there would be a more equal distribution of the nation's wealth. At the same time he identified the weaknesses of the laissez-faire system and focused on its sore spots: the business cycle, market gluts, industrial monopoly, unemployment, poverty, and human misery.

The capitalists were frightened at the prospect of a violent revolution deposing the established order, or of having to tax themselves in order to provide for those less fortunate than themselves. At this juncture, it would seem that the capitalist-individualists and the revolutionary socialists were bound on a collision course which would lead to open conflict. However, during the latter half of the nineteenth century England possessed a group of intellectuals, of whom Beatrice Webb was prominent, who realized that a compromise between the two factions had to be reached in order to avoid a senseless upheaval. They sought to propagate a philosophy which would draw out the best principles of both groups. Beatrice Webb's share in accomplishing this constituted her not inconsiderable contribution to society.

Beatrice Potter was born January 2, 1858, at Standish House, near Gloucester, into a big, happy family of affluence and high social position. Her father was a successful, gregarious mid-Victorian businessman and railroad magnate; her mother, a beautiful, restless, intelligent woman. Beatrice was the next to the youngest in a family of nine daughters. There was a greater span of time between the birthdates of Beatrice and her next older sister (four years) and her younger sister (seven years) than there was between any of the other sisters. A much-longed-for son was born into the family when Beatrice was four. He was a healthy, beautiful child, but he died shortly before his third birthday. Both during and after his short life Beatrice competed jealously and unsuccessfully for her mother's affection, which was showered in great abundance on this baby brother and later on a younger sister. Aloof tolerance characterized this mother-daughter relationship, with neither mother nor daughter recognizing that Beatrice, with her intellectual drive and restless ambition, was the one among all the daughters who most resembled her mother. In the midst of a lively crowd, Beatrice grew up lonely and withdrawn, her mother convinced that "Beatrice is the only one of my children who is below the average in intelligence."[5]

Because of frailty and ill health, the discipline of her sisters' schoolroom was not imposed on her. She had access to a fine home library, of which she wrote years later, "Perhaps the only expenditure unregulated and unrestricted by my mother, she herself being the leading spendthrift, was the purchase or subscription for books, periodicals and newspapers."[6] Her education was determined by her own reading interests, by her association with the domestic servants, and by conversation with many distinguished family guests. Beatrice Potter's closest friend and mentor was Herbert Spencer (1820-1903), a frequent visitor in the Potter home.

Popular philosopher and sociologist, and Beatrice's senior by thirty-eight years, Herbert Spencer had achieved a reputation as a pioneer thinker. An ingenious mind that searched for first principles in the science of life, for laws of intellectual development, and for general principles of education, he sought to unify and coordinate all of science and philosophy. He professed a philosophy of individualism and was always suspicious of reformers. He had a zeal for ascertaining facts and for discovering their relevance to theories of societies, government, and human and animal behavior. Although in her mature scholarship Beatrice rejected Spencer's sweeping generalizations, she never ceased to honor him. She adopted his working techniques, accepted his view of sociology as a universal science, and lived by his belief that one must live for the future of the human race and not for one's own comfort or success. And it was to Spencer's "Religion of Science" that she turned in later years when, in her own religious gropings, her inquiries left her with unresolved doubts.

The year 1882 marked a turning point in Beatrice's life in two ways: her mother died and she began to feel an incipient urge for a vocation. She was then twenty-four years old. She had been prepared for life in upper-class society and she blossomed into a beautiful young woman. "In the seventies and eighties the London [social] season, together with its derivative country-house visiting, was regarded by wealthy parents as the equivalent, for their daughters, of the university education and professional training afforded for their sons, the adequate reason being that marriage to a man of their own or a higher social grade was the only recognized vocation for women not compelled to earn their own livelihood."[7] By reason of her mother's death, her status changed from a relatively inconspicuous member of the Potter family to the mistress of her father's household. As the eldest unmarried daughter, she became her father's companion and part-time secretary until his death in 1892. It would have been easy for her to take advantage of all that social life in London had to offer. Yet she was continually torn with overwhelming ambition for a life of intellectual distinction. She became acutely aware at this stage that her life was "wanting in aim." At a later stage she wrote: "To win recognition as an intellectual worker was, even before my mother's death, my secret ambition. I longed to write a book that would be read; but I had no notion about what I wanted to write. From my diary entries I infer that, if I had followed my taste and my temperament . . . I should have become, not a worker in the field of sociology, but a descriptive psychologist. . . ."[8]

In her groping for a vocation, her friendship with Herbert Spencer became significant. Her study of his works convinced her that social ills could be discovered by fact findng and cured by recommendations for reform based on scientific examination. She decided that the scientific investigation of social institutions was to be her vocation in life. No one who reads her diaries, or her account in her autobiography of her experiences in the ensuing years can doubt that her career choice was deliberate. Nor can one doubt—judging from her meticulous self-analysis, and from her penetrating insights and observations of people and events recorded long before she had acquired professional status as a social investigator—that she would have made a significant contribution to professional psychology had she made that career choice instead. In later years she wrote: "What roused and absorbed my curiosity were men and women, regarded—if I may use an old-fashioned word—as 'souls,' their past and present conditions of life, their thoughts and feelings and their constantly changing behavior. This field of enquiry was not, as yet, recognized in the laboratories of the universities, or in other disciplined explorations of the varieties of human experience. I may add, by the way, that what turned me away from psychology, even the 'psychology' to be found in books, was what seemed to me the barren futility of the text-books then current."[9] And to this, she added: "If I have any vain regrets for absent opportunities it is exactly this: that I grew up to maturity as a sociological investigator without a spell of observation and experiment in the modern science of psychology."[10]

In the 1880s two subjects interested her: poverty and industrial democracy, subjects on which she was to become an authority during her professional career. She recorded later: "Two controversies [were] raging in periodicals and books, and giving rise to perpetual argument within my own circle of relations and acquaintances; on the one hand, the meaning of the poverty of the masses of men; and, on the other, the practicability and desirability of political and industrial democracy as a set-off to, perhaps as a means of redressing, the grievances of the majority of the people."[11]

Intermittently, for five years following 1883, she did volunteer service for the Charity Organization Society [C.O.S.] which embodied the Victorian idea of using charity as an instrument not merely to relieve but to prevent destitution. Her task was to screen those worthy of receiving alms. Such an assignment sounds unbearably condescending today, but it must be remembered that that kind of do-goodism was looked upon as noble back in the 1880s. She recorded later: "In these years of my apprenticeship (1883-1887) the C.O.S. appeared to me as an honest though short-circuited attempt to apply the scientific method of observation and experiment, reasoning and verification, to the task of delivering the poor from their miseries by the personal service and pecuniary assistance tendered by their leisured and wealthy fellow-citizens."[12] At that time she subscribed to the philosophy of the C.O.S. that modern capitalism was the best of all possible ways of organizing industries and services; . . ." and "Barring accident to life and health, which happens to both rich and poor, any family could . . . . maintain its 'independence' from the cradle to the grave, if only its members were reasonably industrious, thrifty, honest, sober and dutiful."[13]

In 1883 (and again in 1886 and 1889) she went to Lancashire under the pseudonym of "Miss Jones"—and assuming the role of a Welsh farmer's daughter—to stay in the house of John Ashworth, a distant cousin, to meet men and women of the working class. These experiences provided her with new insights and her "first chance of personal intimacy, on terms of social equality, with a wage-earning family."[14] She acquired an abiding respect for the simple warmth and honesty of solid working-class people. With growing appreciation she realized the importance of the cooperative movement and of trade unions. She saw the benefit yielded by the Factory Acts and the consequent government inspection, and she wrote: *"Laissez-faire* breaks down, when one watches these things from the inside."[15] In 1885 and for two years thereafter, she assisted in rent collecting and house property management for the working-class flats built by philanthropists to provide cheap and sanitary housing for the poor—work which provided her with firsthand experience and observation of real life in the slums. The expert skills she acquired for direct personal observation and the techniques she developed at this time in the art of interviewing, became basic tools in her pursuit of the scientific method.

In February 1886 she was asked to sign as an article a letter she had sent to the *Pall Mall Gazette* in which she had protested proposed relief works for the unemployed on grounds that they were reforms that would not solve the basic problem of poverty. This article, titled "A Lady's View of the Unemployed," caught the attention of her cousin by marriage, Charles Booth, who had begun work on a monumental study: "Inquiry into the Life and Labour of the People of London."* Booth asked Beatrice to help him with his project.

---

*A reprint of the Booth inquiry, described as the first broad-scale, team-executed urban study, has recently become available, as follows: Charles Booth, et al., *Life and Labour of the People in London.* Five volumes (the fifth is a collection of maps). Reprints of Economic Classics (New York: Kelley, [1889 . . . 1891] 1969), pp. 324, 235, 60, 310, 354.

Charles Booth was one of the first nineteenth-century social investigators to use the scientific methd in social investigation. He sought to discover what were the real facts about the lives of the poor. This was an intellectual position and area of interest that suited Beatrice well, and she joined the project as "an industrious apprentice." Booth believed "the *a priori* reasoning of political economy, orthodox and unorthodox alike, fails from want of reality,"[16] yet he expected his investigations would disprove the Socialists' contention that 25 percent of wage earners were paid insufficient amounts to maintain physical health. His research, in fact, revealed that 30.7 percent of the wage earners were living in a state of chronic destitution or on the line of bare subsistence.[17] The entire Booth inquiry, begun in 1886, resulted in seventeen volumes, publication of which extended over seventeen years.

Beatrice's first recognition as a social investigator came when she published an article, "Dock Life in the East End of London," in 1887 in the leading review *Nineteenth Century*—the result of her investigation for the Booth project. In addition to helping her to acquire confidence in her ability to do the work she believed in, the Booth inquiry had contributed to her intellectual growth in two ways, first, by pointing to the right relation between personal observation and statistical method; and second, by causing her to become aware of the importance of two social institutions, the cooperative and the trade union movement, each of which was to play an important role in her professional career.

Her next investigative project was the sweating system* in the East End tailoring trade and, in order to get local color and to gain insight into the organization of a workshop, she worked in disguise in 1887 as an operator—a "plain trouser hand"—in several workshops. Thereafter additional articles appeared be-

---

*The sweating system occurred in certain occupations where there were no trade unions, where women's and young children's labor predominated, where much of the work was done in the homes of the workers, where often there was much foreign labor, and where the labor was largely unskilled. As a consequence of these conditions low rates of wages, long hours, and bad working conditions prevailed.

tween 1880 and 1890: "The Tailoring Trade of East London" was followed by "Pages from a Work-girl's Diary," and she was called upon to give evidence to the Lord's Committee on the Sweating System. To the question "How would you define the Sweating System?" asked by a member of the Lord's Committee, she answered: "An enquiry into the Sweating System is practically an enquiry into all labor employed in manufacture which has escaped the regulation of the Factory Act and trade unions."[18] And to this, she added: "The sweater is, in fact, the whole nation. The mass of struggling men and women whose sufferings have lately been laid bare are oppressed and defrauded in every relation of life: by the man who sells or gives out the material on which they labor; by the shopkeeper who sells them provisions on credit, or forces them under the truck system; by the landlord who exacts, in return for the four walls of a bedroom or for the unpaved and undrained back-yard, the double rent of workshop and dwelling; and, lastly, by every man, woman, and child who consumes the product of their labor."[19] The philosophy of universality of responsibility for social ills contained in this statement anticipated and was reiterated years later (1909) when, upon being asked by another national committee to explain exactly what was meant by destitution, she replied: "It is in this sense that we are entitled to say that destitution is a disease of society itself."[20] It is evident by 1890 that Beatrice was moving with increasing confidence into the path of her own career. She was seeing social problems in ever larger focus and was being accepted in her own right as an authority on social conditions.

Two other noteworthy events occurred during this decade of professional preparation, each of which is worthy of further attention. First, she wrote and published in 1891 her small but definitive study *The Cooperative Movement in Great Britain,* in which she appraised the merits of consumer democracy; and second, she formulated for her own use "a critique of Political Economy and a constructive view of the functions and methods of Social Science." Each of these will be discussed in turn.

The subject of cooperation was chosen against the advice of both Charles Booth and her friend, "the greatest living econnomist,"[21] Alfred Marshall. They wanted her to make an intensive study of problems related to women's labor, but the topic held no interest for her. Instead, consumer cooperation seemed all-compelling. To her query "Do you think I am equal to it?" Marshall replied with candor: "Now, Miss Potter, I am going to be perfectly frank: of course I think you are equal to a history of Co-operation: but it is not what you can do best . . . . To sum up with perfect frankness: if you devote yourself to the study of your own sex as an industrial factor, your name will be a household word two hundred years hence: if you write a history of Co-operation it will be superseded and ignored in a year or two."[22] But great economists have been proven wrong. Her distaste for the recommended subject was reiterated years later (1918) when, as a member of the War Cabinet Committee on Women in Industry, she wrote that the work of the committee "bores me," and added: "I am not in the least interested in the relation of men's and women's wages."[23]

Part of her resistance to the topic of women's labor was due to the fact that she was at the time (1889) an antifeminist—a position she viewed later as "a false step"[24] and one which placed her in direct opposition to Mrs. Millicent Garrett Fawcett, to whom she wrote a public recantation in 1906.[25] She credited her antifeminism, in part, to the fact that she had deliberately refrained from identifying with any group that had pronounced views about social changes for fear that it would compromise her own independence. Also, she acknowledged that she herself had never "suffered the disabilities assumed to arise from my sex." She observed: ". . . in those days, a competent female writer on economic questions had . . . actually a scarcity value. Thus she secured immediate publication and, to judge by my own experience, was paid a higher rate than that obtained by male competitors of equal standing."[26] On perspective, her preference for studying the cooperative movement reflects the strong bias she displayed throughout her scholarly career for institutional economics.

As preparation for her project she studied the history and theory of cooperation, attended cooperative congresses and observed cooperative practices. In 1891, Beatrice Potter's two hundred and fifty fact-filled pages—*The Cooperative Movement in Great Britain*—was published. She saw cooperation "as one form of democratic association, as one aspect of that larger movement towards an Industrial Democracy which has characterized the history of the British working class of the nineteenth century."[27] Her objective was to probe the "contrast between the wage-earners who had enjoyed the advantages of collective regulation and voluntary combinations, and those who had been abandoned to the rigors of unrestrained individual competition."[28] After describing the condition of the working class in the first decades of the nineteenth century brought about by the Industrial Revolution, she outlined the essential features of consumer and producer cooperation, appraised the principles of "one man, one vote, and no proxies" as "a sound doctrine of suffrage,"[29] and viewed the principle of "dividend on purchase" (i.e., patronage dividends)* as providing "a unique democratic foundation to an industrial organization."[30] She lauded Robert Owen as the founder of the cooperative movement and the father of English socialism, and extolled him for his enlightened policies of labor management, his early (1816) advocacy of factory legislation, his proposals for free and compulsory education, for free libraries, and for public housing.

She noted that the political economists—David Ricardo, John Stuart Mill, John Elliott Cairnes, and others—in their espousal of the self-governing workshop which was based on the theory

---

*Members of a cooperative, who achieve membership by buying one or more shares, are both owners and customers. When receipts from operations exceed expenses, the excess is distributed, not to the members as owners on the basis of the capital invested, but to them as customers in the form of a percentage rebate on purchases. These distributions are not called profits but "patronage dividends." They are equivalent to delayed price reductions. Each member has but one vote, regardless of the number of shares in which he may have invested. "To organize industry from the consumption end, and to place it, from the start, upon the basis of 'production for use' instead of 'production for profit,' under the control and direction, not of the workers as producers, but of themselves as consumers, was the outstanding discovery and practical achievement of the Rochdale Pioneers." (*My Apprenticeship*, p. 370)

that "labor is the source of value," had ignored the fact that "the essential element in the successful conduct of production is the *correspondence* of the application of labor with some actually felt specific desire," i.e., demand. The Rochdale Pioneers, she noted, by method of trial and error had arrived at this truth years before the professional political economists had realized either its nature or its importance. In their emphasis upon consumer democracy, the Rochdale Pioneers "were, in fact, Jevonians before Stanley Jevons, in discovering *that it was in recognized 'utility,' or specific demand, that lay the dominating and delimiting factor of exchange value.* Unlike the self-governing workshops and industrial partnerships, the eleven hundred co-operative stores, and their two great federations, the English and Scottish Wholesale Societies, produce, and cannot help recognizing that they produce, for a known market."[31] Here it is evident that Beatrice Webb saw the importance of consumer demand as a vital market force long before Rosa Luxemburg made it the center of her theory of imperialism or before national income economists were to identify it as the dominant strand in their measurement of aggregate demand.

It is also evident from repeated references that she coined the term "industrial democracy" at this time and viewed it as a goal to which the cooperative movement, working in close alliance with trade unionism, might contribute. And again, the term "collective bargaining" was used here for the first time in its modern connotation when she observed: "Barter between individuals must be superseded by negotiations, through authorized representatives, between groups of workers and consumers. Individualist exchange must follow individualist production, and give place to collective bargaining."[32]

The growth of cooperative enterprise, she acknowledged realistically, had social, administrative, and financial boundaries, and she observed: "The limits of the probable domain of the Co-operative State are now all within sight. Voluntary associations of consumers are practically restricted to the provision of certain articles of personal use, the production of which is not necessarily a monopoly, the consumption of which is not absolutely compulsory, and for which the demand is large and constant. Under the present social system a restricted portion only of the nation is within reach of a social democracy—that intermediate class neither too poor nor too wealthy for democratic self-government."[33] After she had achieved professional maturity in later years, she appraised her early infatuation with cooperation as follows: "To one who had been bred in a stronghold of capitalism, the Consumers' Co-operative Movement seemed a unique romance in the industrial history of the world."[34] It had provided her with valuable insights and an opportunity for personal growth.

The second event of professional significance at this preparatory stage in her career, referred to above, was the attention she gave in 1886-1887 to the study of political economy. She undertook it without enthusiasm, and recorded: "Political economy is hateful—most hateful drudgery. Still, it is evident to me I must master it."[35] Her study culminated in two unpublished essays, one "The History of English Economics;" the other "The Economic Theory of Karl Marx." The first of these took the form of a series of notes "On the Nature of Economic Science," the gist of which appeared much later as an appendix to her first autobiographical volume, *My Apprenticeship* (1926). In it she sought "to understand what are in fact the data upon which political economy is based—what are its necessary assumptions."[36] It provides us with perhaps our best insight into Beatrice Webb—Economist. After concluding her studies in early 1887, she recognized that she had been carried out of her depth as a reasoner and she had come to doubt "the desirability of a water-tight science of political economy."[37] She viewed the sphere of economics as involving studies in social pathology, and concluded that political economy should be treated, not as a self-contained, separate, abstract subject, but as a branch of an all-embracing study of human behavior in society and of social institutions, i.e., as a branch of sociology in the Spencerian sense of that term.

These conclusions reached at this stage of her career were to remain with her to the end of her life, as evidenced by the advice she gave Prime Minister Arthur J. Balfour when he confided to

BEATRICE POTTER WEBB
(1858-1943)
From a photograph
taken in 1916

JOAN ROBINSON
(1903-)

her in 1906 that he was contemplating writing a treatise on economics. She warned him at that time that as a subject economics afforded little challenge, and she suggested that "there were only two things to be done in economics; either a mere sweeping away of fallacies—comparatively easy and somewhat futile . . . or a concrete study of phenomena, say, the course of trade and the effect of different kinds of taxation on it—a task that demanded the devotion of a lifetime and, therefore, one which he could *not* undertake."[38]

"Why not drop, once and for all, the whole notion of a science of Political Economy?" she asked in 1886. "The term itself is a foolish one, which confuses the political with the industrial organization of the community. Even when the modern term Economics is substituted, the 'science' inherits a misleading delimitation of content and a faulty method of reasoning. What needs to be studied are social institutions themselves, as they actually exist or have existed, whatever may be the motive attributed to the men and women concerned; and whatever may be the assumed object or purpose with which these institutions are established or maintained. . . . This study of profit-making capitalism or modern business organization would take its place alongside the separate studies of other social institutions, such as the family; consumers' co-operation; the vocational organizations of the various kinds of producers; local government; the state (or political organization); international relations; the intellectual, aesthetic and religious interests of man, and possibly a host of other departments of what can only be regarded (and may one day be unified) as Sociology."[39]

Pursuing this interdisciplinary view, she continued, somewhat prophetically: "Assuming that we give up the conception of a separate abstract science of Political Economy or Economics, the adjective 'economic' might then be reserved to define the relations between men arising out of their means of livelihood or subsistence; or, to put it in another way, which can be weighed and measured in terms of money—whatever may be the social institution in which these relations occur; exactly as we use the terms racial, political, legal, sporting or sexual, to describe the types of relationships having other objects or ends. Thus we should have the economics of art, or of sport, or of marriage, or of medicine, as the case might be, just as we have the legal aspects of business enterprise, of the family or of municipal government.

"A necessary implication of this new classification would be that what would have to be investigated, described and analyzed are the social institutions themselves, as they exist or have existed, not any assumed 'laws,' unchanging and ubiquitous, comparable with the law of gravity, any failure of correspondence with the facts being dismissed as friction. A second corollary is that these social institutions, like other organic structure, have to be studied, not in any assumed perfection of development, but in all the changing phases of growing social tissue, from embryo to corpse, in health and perversion, in short, as the birth, growth, disease and death of actual social relationships. And their diseases may even be the most interesting part of the study!"[40]

In "The Economic Theory of Karl Marx" Beatrice noted the inadequacy of Marx's labor theory of value as she observed that "value arises in the satisfaction of a desire [demand] by the exercise of a faculty [supply] . . . Price is simply the expression in terms of money of the equation at which a given faculty and a given desire, under given conditions, consent to unite and generate exchange value: . . . Now Karl Marx and his disciples . . . refused to recognize that it took the two to create the third. According to his theory of value, economic faculty, or, as he preferred to call it, 'labor,' is the sole origin of value; he assumed that economic desire is, like the ether, always present; and can therefore be neglected as a joint parent of value. . . . To read Marx, one would think that it was only necessary to make a yard of cloth in order to create exchange value equal to the cost of production, together with a handsome surplus."[41] She called the Marxian world "weird" where "men are automata, commodities have souls; money is incarnated life, and capital has a life-process of its own!" And she added: "This idea of an 'automaton owner,' thus making profit without even being conscious of the existence of any desire to be satisfied, is, to any one who has lived within financial or industrial undertakings, in its glaring discrepancy with facts, nothing less than grotesque."[42]

In the course of these researches, and on introspective reflection, Beatrice realized that she had become a socialist. She had arrived there in recognizable stages, after initial resistance. The conversion had begun in fact in 1883 during her visit to the Lancashire cotton mills when she gained new respect for the Factory Acts and the role of government in their enforcement, and she came to realize that *"Laissez-faire* breaks down, when one watches these things from the inside."[43] Gradually she became convinced that it was impossible to improve the lot of the poor merely by exhortation or entreaty of the industrialists or the workers. From her investigation of the sweated industries she had concluded that sweating occurred as the consequence of allowing uncontrolled free competition under capitalism in any industry which could escape the regulations of the Factory Act and the trade unions. This, she identified as Stage I of her conversion to socialism: "the first stage in the journey—in itself a considerable departure from early Victorian individualism—was an all pervading control, in the interest of the community, of the economic activities of the landlord and the capitalist."[44] Then, after she could see no way out of the the recurrent periods of inflation and depression, with the threat that the regime of private property could not withstand revolution, she arrived at Stage II on her road to socialism. She wrote: "This 'national minimum' of civilized existence, to be legally ensured for every citizen, was the second stage in my progress towards socialism."[45] She came to believe that industry had first to be governed by "democracies of consumers" and later by "democracies of workers." She wrote: "It was this vision of a gradually emerging new social order, to be based on the deliberate adjustment of economic faculty [production] and economic desire [demand], and to be embodied in an interlocking dual organization of democracies of consumers and democracies of producers—voluntary as well as obligatory, and international as well as national—that seemed to me to afford a practicable framework for the future co-operative commonwealth."[46] Her entry in her manuscript diary for February 1, 1890, declared: "At last I am a socialist!"[47]

By 1889 she had decided that the Trade Union Movement would be her next subject of inquiry, and she was, even then, becoming aware of and finding "new meaning in the steady growth of municipal enterprise and other forms of local Government."[48] To these interests she turned, recording in her manuscript diary on August 17, 1889: "Search after truth by the careful measurement of facts is the enthusiasm of my life."[49]

Enough has been written to indicate beyond all doubt that Beatrice Potter, over a span of ten years of arduous self-training, had acquired not only professional competence, but a clear blueprint of the direction her future studies were to take her. But soon a new "enthusiasm" entered her life: Sidney Webb (1859-1947). Beatrice Potter and Sidney Webb met for the first time in January 1890, although each, unbeknown to the other, had admired the other's literary talent before that date. Sidney Webb was a London civil servant, one of the leaders of the Progressive party, who possessed a unique aptitude for documentary research. They were secretly engaged in 1891 and married in 1892. Beatrice recorded in her diary in large letters:

> "Exit Beatrice Potter, July 23rd, 1892.
> Enter Beatrice Webb, or rather Mrs. Sidney Webb, for I lose alas! both names."[50]

Thereafter their careers were combined: politically, through Sidney's eighteen years' administrative service on the London County Council and Beatrice's membership on several governmental committees; and intellectually, through their systematic research and voluminous publications, which resulted in a library of over thirty "solid but unreadable books."[51] Their natures and talents supplemented each other in countless ways. Sidney possessed unique ability for research and writing; Beatrice had unlimited patience and zeal for the study of social institutions and for interviewing their leaders. Both researchers "were democratic collectivists, believing in the eventual triumph, in so far as social environment is concerned, of the principle of equality between man and man."[52] Together they pursued the course which Beatrice had set for herself: first, studies in trade unionism; then local government; and thereafter, poverty.

The first literary output of the Webb "partnership" was *The History of Trade Unionism,* published in the spring of 1894. This was a meticulous eight-hundred-page record of the origin and growth of the trade union movement from its earliest beginnings in Great Britain. The authors saw themselves as guardians of social history as they investigated the confidential records of some of the ancient local societies, convinced "that the Trade Union records contain material of the utmost value to the future historian of industrial and political organization, and that these records are fast disappearing."[53] This volume was, in fact, an historical introduction to their more ambitious study, *Industrial Democracy,* published in 1898, in which they developed their own theory of trade unionism with "a new view of democracy" and "an original set of economic and political hypotheses."[54]

Industrial Democracy was well received upon publication, and it continues to be a useful source book for students in labor economics. Before its publication, however, the authors experienced misgivings of its worth—typical of all authors—as they alternated between predicting that "the worth of our work will be only temporary; all our hypotheses will be either truisms or fallacies in a generation's time," and the opposite extreme of thinking the possible impact of the work would be "as great, in its effect on political and economic thought, as Adam Smith's *Wealth of Nations.*"[55] The nine-hundred-page book was organized in three parts: Trade Union Structure—four chapters; Trade Union Function—thirteen chapters; Trade Union Theory—four chapters; and four Appendices (see page 92). After examining in the concluding chapters of this volume the defects of the wage fund theory which, with its opposition to trade unionism, had prevailed from 1825 to 1875, the authors described their vision that trade unionism should, with technically trained leadership and responsible collective bargaining, assume a special function in the administration of industry of a democratic state and become the civil servant of public welfare. They wrote: "Thus we arrive at the characteristic device of the Doctrine of a Living Wage, which we have termed the National Minimum—the deliberate enforcement, by an elaborate Labor Code, of a definite quota of education, sanitation, leisure, and wages for every grade of workers in every industry. This National Minimum the public opinion of the democratic state will not only support, but positively insist on for the common weal."[56] The National Minimum became a theme central to all of their subsequent research, publications, and policy objectives.

INDUSTRIAL DEMOCRACY

Contents

The new view of democracy which developed from the study of trade unionism, (and Beatrice's previously determined career blueprint) propelled the Webbs into the study of English local government, where they hoped to discover, by studying its structure, function, and social environment, the source of *compulsory* collective action which might provide the mechanism for developing a socialist state. Their research resulted in seven volumes, publication of which extended from 1906 to 1929. Four volumes which appeared before 1920 described the development of English local government from the Revolution of 1688 to 1835, and dealt with the origins of parish, county, manor, borough, and special governmental authorities—an "internal history of the eighteenth century."[57] These were followed (between 1925 and 1929) by three more volumes on the history of the English Poor Law of 1834, and publication of a number of studies on related topics. While the initial attraction of the subject of local government for Beatrice had been the opportunity it afforded to use her talents for social investigation, it was Sidney who set the tone of the work in his zeal for discovering the means by which administrative efficiency in government might best be achieved. She wrote: " . . . if local administration was destined to rival and even to surpass in importance the national Civil Service, it was important to discover by what means the various parishes and counties and municipalities were, in fact governed; how their several administrations had arisen in the past and how they were now developing; and by what extensions and improvements these social institutions could be best fitted for the additional tasks that they would find themselves undertaking."[58]

During this long interval, two other interests, one on economic education, the other on economic policy, occupied them. First, they were instrumental in establishing the London School of Economics and Political Science, which was opened in 1895, and which Beatrice regarded as "perhaps the biggest single enterprise in Our Partnership."[59] In February 1900 she recorded in her diary: "Best of all [Sidney] has persuaded the Royal Commission to recognise economics as a science and not merely as a subject in the Arts Faculty. The preliminary studies for the economics degree will, therefore, be mathematics and biology. This divorce of economics from metaphysics and shoddy history is a great gain. We have always claimed that the study of the structure and function of society was as much a science as the study of any other form of life, and ought to be pursued by the scientific methods used in other organic sciences. Hypothesis ought to be used, not as the unquestioned premiss from which to deduce an unquestioned conclusion, but as an order of thought to be verified by observation and experiment. Such history as will be taught at the School will be the history of social institutions discovered from documents, statistics and the observation of the actual structure and working of living organizations. . . . We see clearly what we intend the School to become and we are convinced that the science will emerge."[60] Decisions in behalf of the School, its finances, its philosophy, its administration and faculty, as well as student conferences and their own lectures there—hers on industrial competition and methods of research*—occupied the years that followed.

The Fabian Society was their second major interest. Beatrice had joined it in 1892; Sidney had been a member since 1885, shortly after the society was founded. They, along with the mercurial George Bernard Shaw, the political theorist Graham Wallas, and others, set its policies and determined the philosophy of the society, which owed a great deal to John Stuart Mill who bridged the gap between Benthamism and socialism. Fabian doctrine espoused a philosophy of gradualism as it sought to permeate existing society with collectivist ideals. "Their summary of Socialism," Beatrice wrote, "comprised essentially collective ownership wherever practicable; collective regulation everywhere else; collective provision according to need for all the impotent and sufferers; and collective taxation in proportion to wealth, especially surplus wealth."[61]

While in the midst of the research on local government, in November 1905, Beatrice was appointed a member of the Royal Commission on the Poor Law and the Relief of Distress†—an assignment that became three years of "hard grind." But this was her opportunity to implement her decision, made long before, to study "the chronic destitutions of whole sections of the people" for which all her previous activities seemed as prolegomena. While Beatrice acknowledged that the twenty-eight commission members were "a body of experts either in poor law administration

---

*These subsequently appeared (1932) in twelve chapters in a volume titled "Methods of Social Study by Sidney and Beatrice Webb" in which were discussed how, by means of observation and analysis, note-taking, interviews, and use of documents, they pursued their specialty of making a comparative study of the working of particular social institutions. An initial chapter is titled: "The Province of Sociology Determined" and a final chapter deals with "The Relation of Science to the Purpose of Life."

†The system of poor relief dating from the Poor Law of 1834, had placed the administration of poor relief in charge of a National Board of Poor Law Commissioners. The country was divided into groups of parishes, in each of which there was a workhouse. No able-bodied poor person could be given relief except by becoming an inmate of a workhouse which served as a "test of destitution."

or social investigation,"[62] severe frictions developed among them over goals and techniques, and ultimately, over recommendations. Thus, two reports, one by the commission's majority, the other, a minority report—the latter a joint Webb product—were published in January 1909.

From the first Beatrice was intent upon investigating the causes, and hence the means, of preventing destitution, not just developing methods of welfare relief. She was professionally aware of the mass of misery, vice, and sordidness in the existing society, and the general policy which she and Sidney espoused was to construct a base to society in the form of a legally enforced "minimum standard of life," the forerunner of today's proposal for a guaranteed annual income. This was to include a national system of old-age pensions to be administered free from any stigma of pauperism; a provision for medical relief to be handled by the public health authorities; and a program for the "social disease of unemployment" that would involve an increase in the personal responsibility of the beneficiaries—the first blueprint of cradle-to-the-grave social security to be implemented within the existing social order.

She described the goals set forth in the Minority Report as follows: "to secure a national minimum of civilized life . . . open to all alike, of both sexes and all classes, by which we meant sufficient nourishment and training when young, a living wage when able-bodied, treatment when sick, and a modest but secure livelihood when disabled or aged."[63] This doctrine of a national minimum of income, health, housing, leisure, and education, in the opinon of Lord Beveridge, the author of the famed Beveridge Report in 1942, was "the principal Webb contribution to social thought."[64] As recognition of her work on the Poor Law Commission, Mrs. Webb was awarded the degree of Doctor of Letters by Manchester University in July 1909.

In order to publicize the message of the Minority Report and to create an awareness of the need to "level up the bottomest layer of society",[65] the Webbs established the National Committee for the Prevention of Destitution.[66] She discovered new talents of leadership in herself—those of lecturer and teacher—as she worked in its behalf. She wrote: "I often wonder whether I like this life of propaganda or not. I enjoy the excitement of successful leadership, I like the consciousness of the use of faculties which have hitherto been unused—the faculty for public speaking and the faculty for organization. On the other hand I feel harassed—I don't like financial responsibilities, I am perpetually haunted by the fear of failure to live up to the position I am forced into. And I grudge the quiet study and thought with its output of big books. I sometimes wonder whether the expenditure of money and energy on mere passing propaganda is as socially useful as research."[67] In this twosome of selfless effort, Beatrice was predominantly the philosopher, while Sidney was the political strategist. It was he who realized that politics was the way to get things done.

The Minority Report campaign launched the earliest systematic attack on "the poverty problem" and generated a belief that society can be spared the vicious circle of degrading poverty by organizing welfare services differently than those created by the Poor Law of 1834. The Webbs sought to convert England to the obligation of preventing destitution, "to *really change* the mind of the people with regard to the facts of destitution, to make them feel the infamy of it and the possibility of avoiding it."[68] The campaign generated venomous controversy between those who would perpetuate the *status quo* and the supporters of the Webbs. Those who attacked their ideas tried to discredit the Webbs by demanding Sidney's resignation of the chairmanship of the London School of Economics. The School was their own cherished educational institution. It had become their dearest "child," and this was an attack below the belt. Beatrice wrote: "It is an awkward corner to turn. We *do* value our connection, and *authoritative* connection with the School, and if Sidney were to retire presently from the chairmanship it would endanger the tie. On the other hand, we value more the continued prosperity of the School so long as it remains unbiased and open to collectivist tendencies."[69] The episode was resolved without damage to the school but the experience convinced them that it was necessary for them "to drop into the background in the School's life."[70] This they did, after 1911, "with placid content," but Sidney continued to support the school's library and endowment.

On December 1, 1912, Beatrice Webb wrote in her diary: "Clifton. St. Vincent's Hotel—Down here for a conference and public meeting on 'War against Poverty' . . . ."[71] This is probably the first use of this now familiar phrase.* It appears in Mrs. Webb's diary on several subsequent dates as she reports the progress of efforts to publicize the crusade for their national minimum of civilized life. In her personal war on poverty Beatrice Webb was well aware of the political implications of the social reform she proposed in the Minority Report, viz., that they were seeking a new synthesis in the reorganization of society "in a nonpartizan and expert form."[72] She asked: "Is public opinion ripe for a synthesis taking the place of chaotic endeavors of public authorities and voluntary agencies?"[73] She was convinced that clearing up the base of society was equally necessary for a sound individualist or a sound socialist state. "The issue," she wrote, "is fairly joined— complete state responsibility with a view of prevention, or partial state responsibility by a new form of relieving destitution unconnected with the poor law, but leaving the poor law for those who fall out of benefit. It is a trial of strength between the two ideas."[74]

State responsibility—complete or partial; poverty—prevention or relief. These were the issues. The controversy continued and by 1913 the issues had deepened. She wrote: "The Labour Movement, indeed the whole of the thinking British public, is to-day the arena of a battle of words, of thoughts and of temperaments. The issue is twofold: are men to be governed by emotion or by reason? Are they to be governed in harmony with the desires of the bulk of the citizens or according to the fervent aspirations of a militant minority in defiance of the will of the majority? Two quite separate questions but each of them raising the same issue: the validity of democratic government."[75]

The Webbs saw destitution as "a disease of society itself" and,

---

*With the passage of the Economic Opportunity Act of 1964, which established the Office of Economic Opportunity, the U.S. Congress declared "war against poverty."

after gathering all available facts by which they could identify a "poverty line," they proposed to convert England to a policy of complete communal responsibility for the prevention of mass destitution in all its forms, whether due to childhood, old age or sickness, illiteracy or unemployment. The Labour Movement became the Labour party; Sidney became its intellectual leader, and Beatrice served on several government committees. Beatrice wrote: "It is annoying not to be able to complete that big task of historical research to which we devoted so much time and money. But there seems to be a clear call to leadership in the Labour and Socialist Movement to which we feel that we must respond."[76] Thus deflected from social investigation, their lives and interests were claimed increasingly by political involvements.

Thereafter all their endeavors were joint endeavors, and their successes and failures were jointly shared. They lived into their eighties—Beatrice died in 1943; Sidney in 1947—and, on the suggestion of George Bernard Shaw, they were honored and buried together in Westminster Abbey in December 1947. Beatrice Webb had collaborated with her husband in writing a massive library of definitive economic volumes; they had nurtured the Fabian Society; they had founded the London School of Economics; they had provided the intellectual leadership in the British Labour party; and they had designed the blueprint for the British Welfare State. Their names and the liberal movement in England were coterminous for over fifty years, and what had begun as an official document in 1909 (the Minority Report), became ultimately, the judgment of the majority of the people. The Welfare State became a fact in Great Britain in 1945.

Times change and our words change: welfare has replaced charity, poverty replaces destitution, the guaranteed annual income takes the place of the national minimum—thus the work of the Webbs continues. In the United States the Economic Opportunity Act of 1964 made official the "War on Poverty" and we continue to strive to implement* the Webbs' 1909 blueprint of a national

---

*The Family Assistance Plan of the 1970s, which incorporates much of what the Webbs conceived in 1909, has yet to be approved.

minimum. With too little "deliberate speed," society has come to realize that "a destitute citizen is a reproach to the economy and of no use to it as a worker to produce, or a market to absorb, saleable goods; ill-health is wasteful and public education is necessary to produce skilled workers and the lower eschelons of the technostructure." However, "the welfare state has very much softened the harshness of raw capitalism and has played a large part in saving it, till now, from the doom that Marx foresaw a hundred years ago."[77]

How, then, to appraise in her own right, the contribution of Beatrice Webb to economics? In judging the contribution of the Webbs, it has become customary to so subordinate Beatrice's personality and contribution to that of Sidney that she is rarely recognized for the strong leadership she actually exerted. Beatrice had arrived at a maturity of scholarship and investigative technique by the time she became associated with the Booth project (1886). She had found a vocation that was right for her. With her zeal for discovering facts and truth, she had become recognized as an eminent social investigator and writer. Her union with Sidney was felicitous for each. Together they became a remarkable team, developing close intellectual and political affinity, yet complementing each other in talents, tastes, and social philosophy. The synthesis of their lives is reflected in Beatrice's words: "On the whole, then, I would advise the brain working woman to marry—if only she can find her Sidney."[78] While it was Beatrice's blueprint for her own work that became the plan for their joint research, it was Sidney's skill in public administration and his selfless devotion to public service that subsequently prevailed. About their joint efforts, Beatrice wrote: ". . . . everyone knows that he is the backbone of the 'Webb' firm, even if I do appear, on some occasions, as the figure-head."[79]

Their contemporaries debated whether Sidney or Beatrice was the more able, "but no conclusions were arrived at, for both were extraordinarily able and yet more extraordinarily diligent."[80] In the words of one contemporary: "Among the acolytes of the Fabian order there is a constant controversy as to which of the two is before or after the other. It is an idle theme, for you can never tell where one ends and the other begins—how much you are yielding to the eloquence of Mrs. Webb, and how much to the suggestion of Mr. Webb. It is she who weaves the spells, but he who forges the bolts. Between them they have an uncanny power of persuasion. Their knowledge overwhelms you, their sweet reasonableness disarms you. You are led captive in the chains of their silken logic, and they have the victories that fall to those whose knowledge is the instrument of relentless purpose, whose patience is inexhaustible and whose urbanity is never ruffled."[81]

Beatrice Webb rarely referred to herself as an economist, and probably seldom thought of herself in that role. Her vision and talents were too broadly gauged to be—in her opinion—so "narrowly" categorized. Her niece, Kitty Muggeridge, refers to her as "the famous sociologist."[82] On one of the rare occasions when Beatrice identified herself with the economics profession, she remarked: "It never occurs to us economists and political science students to imagine that our long-standing study of the complicated structure and function of society fits us to be astronomers or physicists—but the physical science man plunges head foremost into the discussion of our questions, armed with the four rules of arithmetic and the instruments of a laboratory."[83] By implication, this statement clearly identifies her with that goodly company of institutional economists which has included, among others, Max Weber, Thorstein Veblen, Wesley C. Mitchell, and John R. Commons.

As we seek, then, to appraise the contribution to economics made by one of Adam Smith's daughters, we should never underestimate the power of a woman to effect the restructuring of society—when that woman willingly devotes a lifetime to her profession and is joined, emotionally and intellectually, by a gifted and public-spirited man—but it takes a woman of extraordinary willpower and total dedication to her objective to achieve such a result.

NOTES

1. Beatrice Webb, *The Cooperative Movement in Great Britain* (London: Swan Sonnenschein, 1891), p. 2.
2. Webb, *My Apprenticeship* (New York and London: Longmans, Green, 1926), pp. 442, 239.
3. Webb, *The Cooperative Movement*, p. 10.
4. Thomas S. Ashton, "Workers' Living Standards: A Modern Revision," in Philip A. M. Taylor, ed., *The Industrial Revolution in Britain: Triumph or Disaster?* (Boston: D. C. Heath and Company, 1958), p. 46.
5. Webb, *My Apprenticeship*, p. 12.
6. Ibid., p. 55.
7. Ibid., p. 44.
8. Ibid., p. 106.
9. Ibid., p. 133.
10. Ibid., p. 134.
11. Ibid., p. 167.
12. Ibid., p. 189
13. Ibid., p. 200.
14. Ibid., p. 147.
15. Ibid., p. 159.
16. Ibid., p. 216.
17. Ibid., p. 227ff.
18. Ibid., p. 320.
19. Ibid., pp. 322-323.
20. Beatrice Webb, *Our Partnership*, Barbara Drake and Margaret I. Cole, eds. (New York and London: Longmans, Green, 1948), pp. x, 544, 443.
21. Webb, *My Apprenticeship*, p. 337.
22. Ibid., pp. 339-340.
23. Margaret I. Cole, ed., *Beatrice Webb's Diaries 1912-1924*, with an introduction by the Rt. Hon. Lord Beveridge (London and New York: Longmans, Green, 1952), pp. xxvi, 272, 138.
24. Webb, *My Apprenticeship*, p. 341.
25. Webb, *Our Partnership*, p. 362.
26. Webb, *My Apprenticeship*, p. 343.
27. Webb, *Cooperative Movement*, p. v.
28. Webb, *My Apprenticeship*, p. 336.
29. Webb, *Cooperative Movement*, p. 70.
30. Ibid., p. 70.
31. Webb, *My Apprenticeship*, pp. 369-370.
32. Webb, *Cooperative Movement*, pp. 216-217.

33. Ibid., p. 232.
34. Webb, *My Apprenticeship*, p. 367.
35. Ibid., pp. 280-281.
36. Ibid., p. 281.
37. Ibid., p. 282.
38. Webb, *Our Partnership*, p. 354.
39. Webb, *My Apprenticeship*, p. 423.
40. Ibid., pp. 424-425.
41. Ibid., pp. 429-430.
42. Ibid., p. 430.
43. Ibid., p. 159.
44. Ibid., p. 378.
45. Ibid.
46. Ibid., p. 381.
47. Ibid., p. 394.
48. Ibid., p. 380.
49. Ibid., p. 382.
50. Webb, *Our Partnership*, p. 30.
51. Ibid., p. 15.
52. Ibid., p. 87.
53. Sidney and Beatrice Webb, *The History of Trade Unionism* (New York: Augustus M. Kelley, Reprints of Economic Classics, 1965), pp. xv, 784. Preface to the original edition of 1894, p. xiii.
54. Webb, *Our Partnership*, p. 51.
55. Ibid., p. 52.
56. Sidney and Beatrice Webb, *Industrial Democracy* (1913), p. 817. Printed by the Authors for the Trade Unionists of the United Kingdom.
57. Webb, *Our Partnership*, p. 174.
58. Ibid., p. 150.
59. Ibid., p. 84.
60. Ibid., pp. 195-196.
61. Ibid., p. 107.
62. Ibid., p. 321.
63. Ibid., p. 482.
64. Cole, *Diaries*, 1912-1924, p. vii.
65. Webb, *Our Partnership*, p. 428.
66. Ibid., pp. 442-443.
67. Ibid., p. 453.
68. Ibid., p. 435.
69. Ibid., p. 463.
70. Ibid., p. 464.
71. Cole, *Diaries, 1912-1924*, p. 7.
72. Webb, *Our Partnership*, p. 469.

73. Ibid., p. 467.
74. Ibid., p. 476.
75. Cole, *Diaries, 1912-1924,* op. cit., p. 15.
76. Ibid., p. 6.
77. Joan Robinson, *Freedom and Necessity, An Introduction to the Study of Society* (London: George Allen and Unwin, Ltd. 1969), pp. 88, 90.
78. Webb, *Our Partnership,* op. cit., p. 46.
79. Webb, *Our Partnership,* p. 433.
80. Ibid., footnote, p. 59.
81. Ibid., footnote, p. 289.
82. Kitty Muggeridge and Ruth Adam, *Beatrice Webb, a Life 1858-1943* (New York: Alfred A. Knopf, 1968), p. 17.
83. Webb, *Our Partnership,* p. 300.

CHAPTER VI

Joan Robinson
(1903—)

"So here we are! We've managed to survive for some time now, catch as catch can, the fat and the lean, and if the dinosaurs don't trample us to death, and if the grasshoppers don't eat up our garden, we'll all live to see better days, knock on wood. . . . Don't forget that a few years ago we came through the depression by the skin of our teeth! One more tight squeeze like that and where will we be?"
—Thornton Wilder, *The Skin of Our Teeth*

In this second half of the twentieth century economics is no longer the simple, homely set of disconnected truths which it was when Jane Marcet began writing on economics in the early 1800s. Economics has come of age. The discipline today is a closely integrated system of analytical thinking, advancing on the planes of both microeconomics and macroeconomics, intent upon interpreting and guiding the operations of either a planned or a market economy to achieve social goals, yet knowing that its full stature has not yet been reached. "Professionalism, growing in every field, made Victorian amateurism impotent and ridiculous and in pursuing researches more deeply broke up the unity of culture, invented new languages, and created enormous gulfs which the amateurs could neither understand nor bridge."[1] There is no one who has been more responsible for bringing modern economics to its state of professionalism than Mrs. Joan Robinson, a foremost British scholar-economist, professor emeritus of economic theory at the University of Cambridge—the doyenne of her profession.

Up until 1933 there was no understanding and hence no systematic analysis of markets other than those for which the economist's model assumed either an environment of perfect competition or that of pure monopoly. Based on such restricting assumptions, theory, the aim of which is to explain as closely as possible conditions of the real world, did not reflect reality. In the real world firms do compete but they have some control over their market and the prices they charge. There is often a purposeful differentiation of products which introduces an element of monopoly. Furthermore, in industries where producers are few and big, firms behave differently than in those where there are many small producers. The big firms, called oligopolies (or if there are but two, duopolies), restrict output; they charge higher prices and tend not to alter these prices; they make decisions with the expectation that other firms in the industry will react to their decisions and that they in turn must be alert to the decisions of others. In short, oligopolies are dependent on each other and they realize it. The first and foremost contribution of Mrs. Robinson to economics was in this area of imperfect competition. Responding to a suggestion made by Mr. Piero Sraffa in 1926 that "the whole theory of value should be treated in terms of monopoly analysis,"[2] Mrs. Robinson wrote *The Economics of Imperfect Competition* (1933) which precipitated the revision of much of the content and subsequent development of theoretical microeconomics.

Mrs. Robinson's book is not for the beginner. It employs rigorous abstract analysis and assumes a high level of competence in economic theory. The author herself acknowledged, somewhat apologetically, that "the level of abstraction maintained in this book is distressingly high."[3] With intricate diagrams—many of which were then new to economic science—mathematical demonstrations, and closely reasoned interpretations, she provided a statement of conditions of market equilibrium applicable to the whole spectrum of market structures: competition, monopoly, or to any intermediate situation of "monopolistic" or "imperfect" competition.

Mrs. Robinson stated that her main theme was the analysis of value, but her course led inevitably into such topics as price discrimination, monopoly, monopsony (i.e., monopoly buying, a word introduced by Mrs. Robinson), marginal productivity, market exploitation, and the concept of the "kinked" demand curve. She emphasized that while the type of competition that characterizes oligopolies is different from the competition conceived by Adam Smith and other classical economists, the oligopolies' motivation for profits is no less strong, and the mechanism by which they make their decisions is quite similar to the analysis which had previously been applied exclusively to perfectly competitive conditions. "Thus," she wrote, "the common-sense rule that the individual will equate marginal gains (whether of utility or revenue) with marginal cost, applies to monopsony, to monopoly, and to perfect competition. . . . The cases which arise in perfect competition are only special cases of the general rule that the individual will equate marginal cost to him with marginal gain."[4]

Mrs. Robinson's explanation of the price behavior of oligopolies was made graphic[5] by the so-called kinked demand curve, which shows that if an oligopoly tries to raise prices the volume of its sales will decline sharply as it loses customers to rival firms who do not follow its price increase; while if it lowers prices it does not gain new customers because competing firms will usually lower their prices too. Hence oligopolies try to rid themselves of uncertainty by means of cartel and price-leadership agreements, so their prices become rigid and noncompetitive. Oligopolies do compete in other ways, such as service or quality, but for them to compete in prices is impractical. In the author's words: ". . . any conventional pattern of behavior which establishes itself amongst an imperfectly competitive group provides a stable result. So long as all adhere to the same set of conventions each can enjoy his share of the market, and each can imagine that he is acting according to the strict rules of competition, though in fact the group as a whole, by unconscious collusion, are imposing a mild degree of monopoly upon the market."[6]

It was further demonstrated, within the framework of orthodox theory, that wages under imperfect competition are normally less than the value of the marginal product of labor.

Whether or not she made a "wrong turning," as she wrote and

thought some years later,[7] when she made her initial choice for research between expanding Marshall's static rather than his dynamic analysis, Mrs. Robinson's pioneer work in imperfect competition did provide a major breakthrough in theoretical economics by revitalizing price theory, stimulating research into various aspects of microeconomic behavior, and causing analysis of market behavior once again to become relevant to the real economy—a world populated by oligopolies. Her book has been acclaimed by the economics profession as an outstanding economic event, one which set economic theory on a new road, one with a more useful destination. Its substance is incorporated in every comprehensive modern economics text.

As has happened more than a few times in the development of economics, more than one researcher, each unknown to the other, were exploring the same virgin territory simultaneously and produced their conclusions at almost exactly the same time. The theory of imperfect competition was also explored by Edward H. Chamberlin (1899-1967) in a Harvard University dissertation, titled *The Theory of Monopolistic Competition* and published in 1933. At a much later date with reference to some other equally fortuitous parallels in economics, Professor Robinson wrote: "Such coincidences . . . are an indication that a stage has been reached in the evolution of a subject when there is a particular next step that has to be taken."[8] Thus the two authors, Chamberlin and Robinson, share credit for their research in this area. Both started from the premise that aspects of monopoly were more typical than exceptional. Professor Robinson concerned herself with competition among the few, while Chamberlin concerned himself with monopoly among the many. Time has proven Professor Robinson's approach the more realistic. To a considerable extent the two works parallel and supplement each other.

In a new preface to a second (1969) edition of her book, Professor Robinson observed that while the work presented a static approach within the short-period aspect of competition, its strong points were, in fact, negative. First, by showing that perfect competition cannot prevail in manufacturing industry, it demonstrates that price does not equal marginal cost, and thereby undermines the traditional teaching orthodoxy which rests upon the assumptions of the perfectly competitive market. Second, it shows that consumer's sovereignty can never prevail so long as market initiative, through the use of vast advertising and marketing budgets, lies with the producer. And third, with oligopolists in command of the market, it proves that wages are not equal to but are in fact considerably less than the value of the marginal product of labor, thus negating equity in the distribution of income. Each of these points generates arguments for the need of a new approach to economic teaching, one that acknowledges that a new economic structure has replaced the assumptions on which the ideology of laissez faire was based. Her plea for a revision of economic theory based on realism is a thesis she returns to repeatedly in subsequent works.

The Economics of Imperfect Competition was only the beginning of a succession of distinguished contributions to economics by Mrs. Robinson. If she had written nothing else, this book would have merited lasting fame for her, and appreciation from her profession. But from here she has continued to explore and enrich the subject of economics by producing studies in many significant areas of contemporary economic interest. Her works constitute virtually a one-author economics library. They include the following:

Introduction to the Theory of Employment	(1937)
Essays in the Theory of Employment	(1937)
An Essay on Marxian Economics	(1942)
The Accumulation of Capital	(1956)
Exercises in Economic Analysis	(1960)
Essays in the Theory of Economic Growth	(1962)
Economic Philosophy	(1962)
Economics: An Awkward Corner	(1967)
Freedom and Necessity	(1969)
Economic Heresies	(1971)

In addition to the above, several of which have appeared in second editions, three volumes of *Collected Economic Papers*—

Volume I with twenty-five articles, Volume II with twenty-one articles, and Volume III with twenty-four articles—have appeared in 1951, 1960, and 1965 respectively, with a continuing output of scholarly articles in contemporary journals.

Soon after the publication in January 1936 of *The General Theory of Employment, Interest and Money by* John Maynard Keynes, Mrs. Robinson established herself as an ardent disciple of Keynes and an eloquent interpreter of this volume which was destined to become an indestructible landmark in economic theory. *Introduction to the Theory of Employment* (1937) provides one of the first explanations of elements of Keynes's analysis as it deals with such topics as investment and saving, the multiplier, employment and unemployment, prices and the rate of interest. In the same year (1937) her *Essays in the Theory of Employment* appeared in which she used Keynesian theory to interpret several particular problems and found application of Keynesianism to some problems beyond which Keynes himself was aware. Here she abandons concern for the Keynesian beginner, and in thirteen essays applies the full reach of her analytical skills to examine, with highly specialized techniques, such topics as full employment, mobility of labor, several causes and remedies for unemployment, disinvestment, and the concept of zero saving. She recognized that Keynes's *General Theory* had been concerned chiefly with short-run analysis, and at this early date, in an essay titled "The Long-Period Theory of Employment," she set about in highly abstract terms "to outline a method by which Mr. Keynes's system of analysis may be extended into the regions of the long period and by which it may become possible to examine the long-period influences which are at work at any moment of time."[9]

Having observed at first hand at the University of Cambridge the development of Keynes's economic thinking from his *Treatise on Money* (1930) to the *General Theory,* she was well equipped to interpret, not only the details of his thinking in terms of the published writings,* but to foresee where the further pursuit of

---

*In an essay titled "Kalecki and Keynes" published in 1964, Professor Robinson argues convincingly that "without any contact either way,"

his ideas would have led him if not cut short by his death in 1946. Specifically, she concentrated on extending the Keynesian model to the fields of economic growth and international trade, subjects of ongoing interest to Professor Robinson, which, as we shall see, she continues to explore.

The final paper in *Essays in the Theory of Employment,* titled "Some Reflections on Marxist Economics," is a searching inquiry into the contradictory position in which a person finds himself, who simultaneously espouses Marxism and Say's Law, the one developing a theory to explain unemployment, while the other assumes that unemployment cannot exist. It is a natural transition from this essay to *An Essay on Marxian Economics* (1942) in which Mrs. Robinson applied modern academic methods of analysis to Marxism. Concerned as she is with the future course of economic theory, she sought, by revealing the harmonies and conflicts between Marxism and academic economics, to discover a basis for their synthesis. First she traced the essentials of Marxian doctrine, and then interpreted the "mysticism" of his specialized vocabulary in terms of what she understood "Marx to have been saying in language intelligible to the academic economist."[11] "The substance of Marx's argument," she remarked, "is far from being irrelevant to the modern situation, but the argument has become incompatible with its verbal integument."[12] On the other hand, she observed "that modern academic economics has something to offer to the Marxists."[13] On the whole, in this essay Mrs. Robinson regards Marx as a great genius, though a human being capable of making mistakes. She confirmed this opinion when, at

---

Michal Kalecki had found in the theory of effective demand the same solution to relieve prolonged unemployment as Keynes. Kalecki emphasized the influence of investment on the share of profits and brought imperfect competition into the analysis. Here once again, Professor Robinson states, "Two thinkers, from completely different political and intellectual starting points [had] come to the same conclusion,"[10] to which she added subsequently: "Kalecki's version was in some ways more truly a *general* theory than Keynes's" (see footnote 85 below). Claim for Kalecki's priority of publication rests upon the argument presented in his book *Essays in the Theory of Business Cycles* published in Poland in 1933 and now made available in his collected works by Cambridge University Press.

a later date, she wrote: "For a discussion of the questions nowadays found to be interesting—growth and stagnation, technical progress and the demand for labor, the balance of sectors in an expanding economy—Marxian theory provides a starting point where academic teaching was totally blank. . . . Marx, as a scientist, proclaimed this grand program, and made an impressive start upon it. But it got very little further. A school of thought flourishes when the followers continuously revise and sift the ideas of the founder, test his hypotheses, correct his errors, reconcile contradictions in his conclusions, and adapt his method to deal with fresh matter. It takes a great genius to set a new subject going; the disciples must admire, even reverence, the master, but they should not defer to him. On the contrary, they must be his closest critics."[14]

While Mrs. Robinson noted in the 1942 essay "that no point of substance in Marx's argument depends on the labour theory of value,"[15] she also pointed out that Marx implements his bitter hatred of oppression by using terminology which "derives its force from the moral indignation with which it is saturated."

Again Marx's search for a theory of causation of economic crises and his analysis of the balance between capital-good and consumption-good industries foreshadows Keynes's theory of employment[16] by means of which Marx's writing can be made comprehensible and currently relevant. Once again Mrs. Robinson recognized the importance of long-period analysis, and concluding on this note, she wrote: "The theory of short-period fluctuations in effective demand, opened up by Mr. Keynes's *General Theory,* has already made great progress. Marx was mainly concerned with long-run dynamic analysis, and this field is still largely untilled. . . . Marx, however imperfectly he worked out the details, set himself the task of discovering the law of motion of capitalism, and if there is any hope of progress in economics at all, it must be in using academic methods to solve the problems posed by Marx."[17] To this challenge Mrs. Robinson herself responded in her next major treatise.

The topic of the accumulation of capital has been one of central concern to economists from Adam Smith to the present because the subject is basic to any examination of economic growth and development. Book II of Adam Smith's *The Wealth of Nations*, and specifically Chapter 3 of Book II, were both titled "The Accumulation of Capital." Smith viewed capital accumulation, the division of labor, and a widening market as the chief sources of economic growth. We have seen that Rosa Luxemburg acknowledged the importance of the topic to Marxism because she wrote her major economic treatise under the same title. Mrs. Robinson wrote a penetrating interpretation and critique of Rosa Luxemburg's book in 1951, which appeared as an introduction to its English translation.[18] (See above, page 69.)

In 1956 Mrs. Robinson produced a comprehensive work of her own under the same title, a work which requires the best analytical equipment and diligence the student of economics can bring to it. *The Accumulation of Capital* (1956) discusses the dynamic long-run consequences of the accumulation of capital that investment in the short run brings about. Here the interplay of capital accumulation and technical progress is analyzed in relation to the rate of growth and the rate of profit. It was found that the success of capitalism depends on technical progress, which may take the form of increases in productivity, most frequently embodied in new types of equipment, which, in turn, requires capital accumulation at an appropriate rate.

The author began by defining the familiar concepts and categories required for the analysis of accumulation (i.e., investment) —income, wealth, capital, money, purchasing power, equilibrium —and found their meanings "elusive," "not very precise," "paradoxical," "metaphysical," but nonetheless "useful." For purposes of her own analysis she dissected the term "equilibrium" (which concept she deemed "treacherous"), and introduced several new terms which reappear in several of her later writings:

a state of *tranquillity:* When an economy develops in a smooth regular manner without internal contradictions or external shocks, so that expectations based upon past experience are very confidently held, and are in fact constantly fulfilled and therefore renewed as time goes by.[19]

a condition of *lucidity:*   when everyone is fully aware of the situation in all markets, and understands the technical properties of all commodities, both their use in production and the satisfaction that they give in consumption.[20]

a situation of *harmony:*   when the rules of the game are fully understood and accepted by everyone, in which no one tries to alter his share in the proceeds of the economy, and all combine to increase the total to be shared.[21]

The author acknowledged that "it is only necessary to describe these conditions to see how remote they are from the states in which actual economies dwell. Capitalism, in particular, could never have come into existence in such conditions, for the divorce between work and property, which makes large-scale enterprise possible, entails conflict; and the rules of the game have been developed precisely to make accumulation and technical progress possible in conditions of uncertainty and imperfect knowledge. Yet too much disturbance, deception and conflict would break an economy to pieces. The persistence of capitalism till to-day is evidence that certain principles of coherence are imbedded in its confusion."[22]

Thereafter, in order to examine accumulation in the long run, and to discover those "certain principles of coherence," she built a succession of carefully controlled models, progressing from one based on highly simplified assumptions to others of increasing complexity, with "the whole argument . . . set out, as far as possible, as an analytical construction, with a minimum of controversy."[23]

In order to identify the conditions necessary for harmonious development Mrs. Robinson introduced the concept of *a golden age,* a condition of neutral technical progress, which she acknowledges to be "a mythical state of affairs not likely to obtain in any economy."[24] It occurs, she wrote, "when technical progress is neutral, and proceeding steadily without any change in the time pattern of production, the competitive mechanism working freely, population growing . . . at a steady rate and accumulation going on fast enough to supply productive capacity for all available labour. [Then] the rate of profit tends to be constant and the level of real wages to rise with output per man. There are then no internal contradictions in the system."[25] Neutral technical progress occurs when the technical progress incorporated in new capital equipment is neither capital using nor capital saving. While it does not alter the capital/labor ratios in the economy, it increases the productivity of labor uniformly in the entire economy. With capital accumulation progressing at a steady rate and with no political disturbances, the system develops smoothly. "Total annual output and the stock of capital (valued in terms of commodities) then grow together at a constant proportionate rate compounded of the rate of increase of the labour force and the rate of increase of output per man."[26] In a series of interim conclusions, she found that "The rate of technical progress and the rate of increase of the labour force . . . govern the rate of growth of output of an economy that can be permanently maintained at a constant rate of profit."[27] Thus, "When the potential growth rate is being realized the economy is in a golden age."[28]

The book continues in its 435 pages and 36 chapters with intricate discussions of prices, wages, investment, and profits in the short run, and with separate sections dealing with finance, land, and international trade—the whole a tour de force of precision thinking by means of deductive analysis. Mrs. Robinson's analytical work on the importance of technical progress to economic development, published in 1956, is notable since good empirical studies on the relative importance of increased capital per worker and technical progress were not published until the period 1962-1966.[29]

Utilizing some of the concepts developed in *The Accumulation of Capital* Mrs. Robinson turns in *Exercises in Economic Analysis* (1960) from writing for members of the economics profession to writing for potential future members of the profession, i.e., students. Much of the analysis of the earlier work, with its specialized vocabulary and its methodology of model building, reappears here. In the *Exercises* the author produced a unique textbook that demonstrates without definitions or diagrams how the principles of economic science can be developed from tightly knit reasoning and rational constructs. Without attempting to explain analytical method, she demonstrates it. Instead of supplying graphs, she gives instructions to the student on how to construct them, so the student can see not only their derivation, but the value of using graphical analytical techniques. This work is not intended to be an exhaustive treatise as are most modern introductory texts, yet it covers a broad spectrum of both macro- and microeconomics. Mrs. Robinson states that she tried merely to show the student "how propositions in economic theory are arrived at so that he can carry on for himself where the book leaves off."[30] Advanced undergraduates find its do-it-yourself approach to economic analysis challenging and enjoyable.

The book consists of five major sections: 1) Production and Accumulation; 2) Accumulation and Distribution; 3) An Exchange Economy 4) Capitalist Industry; and 5) Rational Price System. Certain universal economic problems are illustrated by means of three hypothetical societies: 1) a society of free peasant families; 2) a pure socialist economy; and 3) a pure capitalist system. Since the capitalist economy is of central interest, the other two are considered chiefly for purposes of contrast.

Acknowledging that *The Accumulation of Capital* had been "found excessively difficult,"[31] and oppressed by the awareness that "accepted teaching was still doped by static equilibrium analysis,"[32] Mrs. Robinson returned to this theme in *Essays in the Theory of Economic Growth* (1963). Here, determined "to get economic analysis off the mud of static equilibrium theory"[33] she developed her theme in four essays: I. Normal Prices, II. A Model of Accumulation, III. A Model of Technical Progress, and IV. A Neo-Neoclassical Theorem.

In the whole she moves successively from an analysis of equilibrium prices in classical and neoclassical microeconomic models to an analysis of the concept of general equilibrium in classical, neoclassical, and Keynesian macroeconomic models. The concept of equilibrium, a taken-for-granted tool in economics, is a critical focus of her attention. Equilibrium in neoclassical microeconomic analysis is viewed as a condition in which each employer of factors of production seeks to minimize the cost of his production and to maximize his own return, each unit of a factor seeks the employment that maximizes its income, and each consumer plans his consumption to maximize his utility. There is one equilibrium position in which each individual, assumed to be gifted with perfect foresight in each of his several economic relationships, is doing the best for himself so that no one has any incentive to move. In relation to this analysis Mrs. Robinson observed "that equilibrium prices are never likely to be ruling at any particular moment,"[34] and asked "What meaning can we attach to the conception of a position which is never reached at any particular moment of time but yet which exists only in virtue of the fact that the parties concerned believe, at each moment of time, that it will be reached in the future?"[35]

At a later date she stated that "The concept of equilibrium, of course, is an indispensable tool of analysis. . . . But to use the equilibrium concept one has to keep it in its place, and its place is strictly in the preliminary stages of an analytical argument, not in the framing of hypotheses to be tested against the facts, for we know perfectly well that we shall not find facts in a state of equilibrium."[36] At the same time she answered her own question posed above, with the following sarcasm: "Logical structures of this kind have a certain charm. They allow those without mathematics to catch a hint of what intellectual beauty means. This has been a great support to them in their ideological function. In the face of such elegance, only a philistine could complain that the contemplation of an ultimate stationary state, when accumulation has come to an end, is not going to help us very much with the problems of today.[37]

In relation to general equilibrium in microeconomic analysis, traditional economics has long taught that "At any moment there is a certain equilibrium position towards which the system is tending, but the position of equilibrium shifts faster than the system can move towards any one position of equilibrium."[38] Mrs. Robinson promptly went beyond this, and observed: "An economy may be in equilibrium from a short-period point of view and yet contain within itself incompatibilities that are soon going to knock it out of equilibrium."[39] She reasoned that "No one would deny that to speak of a tendency towards equilibrium that itself shifts the position towards which it is tending is a contradiction in terms."[40]

Thereafter, the concept of equilibrium in her analysis becomes a dynamic concept, influenced by seven independent determinants which are established by the rules and motives governing human behavior in the economy under examination. For a free economy, these are: 1) technical conditions; 2) investment policy; 3) thriftiness conditions; 4) competitive conditions; 5) the wage bargain; 6) financial conditions; and 7) the initial stock of capital goods and the state of expectations formed by past experience. When these determinants combine in a fortuitous manner to achieve smooth, steady growth with full employment, "a golden age," that state of mythical equilibrium, results. The unlikelihood of this occurring in a free market economy is obvious. "To set out the characteristics of a golden age by no means implies a prediction that it is likely to be realized in any actual period of history. The concept is useful, rather, as a means of distinguishing various types of disharmony that are liable to arise in an uncontrolled economy."[41]

Subsequently, in a succession of models using highly abstract analysis, she demonstrates how each of the several determinants of equilibrium affect the level of operation of the economy. In "A Neo-neoclassical Theorem" the author arrived at the proposition which states that "When the conception of the rate of profit determined by the rate of accumulation of capital and thriftiness conditions is combined with the conception of a choice of technique from a given spectrum of possibilities, it can be seen that the highest rate of output of consumption goods is achieved when the rate of profit on capital is equal to the rate of accumulation."[42] Later she simplified this to state that enterprise, consumer and general equilibrium, could be achieved when "the rate of profit on capital is equal to the rate of growth of the economy"[43] but she observed that actual conditions are far from realizing this balance. She cautioned that it is not legitimate to draw practical conclusions from such highly abstract and theoretical explorations as had been conducted, but she could not refrain from observing that "if there is any rough correspondence between reality and the type of analysis here set out, the fact that the rate of profit on capital may be of the order of 15 or 20 per cent in an economy that is growing at the rate of 2 or 3 per cent per annum, does suggest some interesting lines of thought."[44]

From its inception economics has been a moral science. Adam Smith's *Theory of Moral Sentiments* (1758) preceded *The Wealth of Nations* by eighteen years and it is doubtless true to say that the "father" of economics thought of himself more as a moral philosopher than as an economist. Every economic treatise has had an overt or an implicit ethical message in that each, in its own way and within its accepted ideology, has sought a way to preserve and augment productive capacity for the future. From the first, Mrs. Robinson was aware that "it is not possible to describe [an economic] *system* without moral judgments creeping in"[45] and "because the subject is necessarily soaked in moral feelings, judgment is coloured by prejudice."[46]

This theme appears repeatedly in Mrs. Robinson's writings. In *The Economics of Imperfect Competition* she examined "The Moral of Price Discrimination"—the title of Chapter 16. In "An Economist's Sermon," the penultimate essay in *Essays in the Theory of Employment,* she wrote, in comment upon the argument that an equal distribution of income would do little to reduce poverty: "For my own part I have never been able to see the *moral* force of this argument."[47] She suggested instead that with redistribution, the average standard of living should rise as the aggregate of consumption rose and unemployment fell. In *An Essay on Marxian Economics* she observed that Marx's terminology "derives its force from the moral indignation with which it is saturated," as illustrated by the prominence he gave to such terms as "exploitation," "surplus value," and "unpaid labor," but when his language is defused, she finds "there is a certain moral affinity between the modern theory and Marx's analysis."[48] In *The Accumulation of Capital* she wrote that the "viability [of an economy] depends upon the moral ideas of its inhabitants."[49]

Mrs. Robinson turned her full attention to this theme in *Economic Philosophy* (1962). Observing that "some standard of morality is necessary for every social animal"[50] she found that morality, which is derived neither from religion nor from reason, but from a physical base, arises out of biological necessity—"the necessity for each to be subject to the good of all."[51] She explored the origin of conscience and found it as indigenous to the human brain as a propensity to learn a language. What, she asked, is the content of our ethical feelings? "The content of a conscience, like the particular language that is learned, depends upon the society in which the individual grows up."[52] "Any economic system requires a set of rules, an ideology to justify them, and a conscience in the individual which makes him strive to carry them out."[53]

What then are the moral rules which find expression in our ideology? In a series of brilliant and penetrating chapters Mrs. Robinson examines successively the role in classical economics of the concept of "value": "one of the great metaphysical ideas in economics";[54] the role in the neoclassics of "utility": "a metaphysical concept of impregnable circularity," one which justified laissez-faire ideology and led to the sterile concept of equilibrium; and the metaphysical content of Keynesianism with its special emphasis on "full employment": "the great ideology-bearing concept in the *General Theory*"[55] which, while becoming an end in itself, provided a "new defence of *laisser faire.*"[56]

Each of these in its own way, the author indicates, has either had its intended meaning distorted (e.g., value, by the theory of relative prices or by the labor theory of value), or has led us astray (e.g., utility and equilibrium). As we emerge from their hypnotic influence, we have been "left in the uncomfortable situation of having to think for ourselves."[57] Thereafter the ideology of economic growth, which "marks, as it were, the watershed between Keynesian and modern analysis" took over. But growth for what? (The same question has been asked for "work," "GNP," "employment," and "aggregate demand.") At a somewhat later date Mrs. Robinson wrote: "Yet, apart from the requirements of the balance of trade, growth for its own sake is not a rational objective of policy. It would be a rational use of growing resources to remove poverty, to clear up the hideous legacy of the industrial revolution, to build the schools and hospitals and train the personnel that the social services urgently require, as well as to modernize industry. It would be necessary to carry out technical and social research to see what needs to be done. The rate of return in benefit to society of investment would certainly be shown to be very high, so that such a policy would require growth for a long time to come. Growth should be the consequence, not the aim, of rational economic policy."[58]

Even so, there still remains a searching question as to growth, one that is basic to dynamic long-run analysis and important to both developed and underdeveloped nations, as each seeks to plot its course, viz., What governs the overall rate of accumulation of capital? Earlier answers such as those provided by Marx (the innate nature of the capitalist) or by Keynes (animal spirits) are unsatisfying. Mrs. Robinson observed: "To understand the motives for investment, we have to understand human nature and the manner in which it reacts to the various kinds of social and economic system in which it has to operate. We have not got far enough yet to put it into algebra."[59] Certain questions in, or related to, economics cannot be answered by pure science. Many economists, but not Mrs. Robinson, disregard these questions.

Unfortunately or realistically, Mrs. Robinson found the choices for the future that must be made, whether in behalf of world policy, national policy, or the internal operation of the economy itself, must be sought within ideological frameworks that are complex and often contradictory. In a world where "a genuinely universalist point of view is very rare,"[60] international problems must be resolved within the compass of "one solid lump of ideology"—nationalism. National policy, on the other hand, is formulated largely within a laissez-faire ideology. Its bias dominates our thinking when we seek solution, for example, to the problem of poverty amidst plenty, or agreement on what is a well-balanced pattern of private and public investment. Nor do we have a clear-cut philosophy to guide individual decision-makers in an industrial economy as they flounder in confusion between those courses of action that yield the greatest profit and those that yield the greatest social benefit. To these matters Mrs. Robinson finds no pat solutions. Dealing with them in her final chapter in *Economic Philosophy,* "What are the Rules of the Game?", she concludes: "The moral problem is a conflict that can never be settled. Social life will always present mankind with a choice of evils. No metaphysical solution that can ever be formulated will seem satisfactory for long. The solutions offered by economists were no less delusory than those of the theologians that they displaced."[61]

Throughout her professional career Mrs. Robinson has been primarily a pure scientist, an economist's theorist, a professional concerned with development of abstract economic analysis, intent upon maintaining ethical neutrality as she dealt with matters of current policy. The titles in three volumes of collected papers, containing twenty-five, twenty-one, and twenty-four papers respectively, and published in 1951, 1960, and 1965, confirm her concern for advancing the reaches of her profession, although several papers deal with topics of current policy. By 1962 she had reached the conclusion that "As a pure subject [economics] is too difficult to be a rewarding object for study . . . It would never have been developed except in the hope of throwing light upon questions of policy."[62]

Applied economics thus claimed her attention in her next book, *Economics: An Awkward Corner* (1967). Here she abandons the impersonality of the rigid abstract analysis that dominates her previous studies and concerns herself with contemporary policy. In a series of six short essays on Income and Prices; The Balance of Trade; International Finance; Employment and Growth; Monopoly and Competition; and Work and Property, she reveals her social philosophy as that of a modern humanist as she discusses, with particular reference to Great Britain, the current status of these several issues and finds the British economy at "an awkward phase in the continuing process of historical development."[63]

Many of her observations are as applicable to the economy of the United States as they are to that of Great Britain. In both societies ideological contradictions abound. The ideology of laissez faire survives in spite of the evident need for government planning to maintain employment goals, satisfactory levels of money incomes and prices, and a balance of international payments. Modern society, with its vast productive capacity, and potential for less social inequality, employs mere palliatives to avoid greater equality of income distribution because we have "no philosophy to guide us in sharing it out."[64] The ideology of economic growth, "designed to prevent us from asking what we want to do with it," and dependent as it is upon an ever-expanding effective demand to maintain prosperity, supports such anomalies as toleration of vast expenditures for armaments, multibillion dollar outlays for space exploration, or a compounding increase in population to provide an ever-expanding market. We ask, with no readily available answer, whether prosperity can be maintained without these contrived stimulants.

Such are the contradictions of modern capitalism, and, Professor Robinson writes, they "arise from the need to readjust the organization of Society to the fantastic capacity for production of material wealth that the application of science to technology has made possible."[65] Economics can point the way, but it cannot impose the correctives. "The obstacles to such schemes are neither technical nor legal. They lie in the political opposition that could be rallied against them at home and the threat of flights of capital and capitalists to more congenial shores."[66] Truly, economics is in "an awkward corner." "Perhaps in the end," Mrs. Robinson concludes, "the facts of life, like a sheepdog with an awkward flock, will finally nudge democracy towards common sense."[67]

From a different approach this theme is continued in *Freedom and Necessity, An Introduction to the Study of Society* (1969). Here is a panoramic view of the role of economics in human history. It is a compact (124 pages), wide-ranging, and brilliant social history of economic science. As an economic anthropologist, Professor Robinson searches in early chapters for the reasons for species survival (pressure of technical conditions, not heredity), and examines the ways by which various species have developed skills needful for survival, for learning correct social behavior ("the basic moral problem"), and for establishing a hierarchy of ranks. There follows, in the tradition of the nineteenth-century philosophical radicals, a search for origins: the concept of private property; the organization of warfare; the economics of capital accumulation and investment; the rationalization of race and social class; notions of democracy and national patriotism. The interplay of freedom and necessity "which is the characteristic of human life,"[68] is found to express itself in many ways in the course of societal evolution as we have endeavored to resolve the endless conflict between the freedom of the individual and the necessity of the group.

She observes that "there are three characteristics of the modern age which distinguish it from the past—the hypertrophy of the nation state . . . the application of science to production and the penetration of money values into every aspect of life," and she continues: "Scientific discoveries were still often made in the pursuit of knowledge for its own sake, but the profit motive provided digestive organs that absorbed them into productive technology. The spiral action of technical development was set going which has been spinning ever since at a more and more vertiginous rate."[69]

Thereafter, in brilliant vignettes[70] she identified successive views of social progress as held among others by Ricardo, Marx, and Marshall—the latter's "vision of industry at the service of mankind" having been distorted into a "nightmare of terror" by modern militarism and war. In the course of exploring the contemporary scene, she writes: ". . . the profit motive contains no mechanism to ensure that technical progress will take digestible forms. . . . Modern capitalism is well adapted to produce fabulous technical successes but not to provide the basis for the noble life accessible to all that Marshall dreamed of."[71] She continues incisively: "The requirements of the warfare state and the welfare state meet in the export of armaments, which keep industry in ex-imperialist countries prosperous and permit enmities in the ex-colonial countries, which were frozen at the level of bows and arrows or flintlocks, to break out with bombs and tanks."[72]

After examining how some other modern economies—Sweden, Soviet Russia, Maoist China, and new nations of the Third World— have organized themselves, she remarks that the time has come when we should advance into a new stage of social self-consciousness beyond the "first-degree" ideology based upon laissez-faire profit motivation. "The task of social science now," she writes, "is to raise self-consciousness to the second degree, to find out the causes, the mode of functioning and the consequences of the adoption of ideologies, so as to submit them to rational criticism. Only too often would-be scientists are still operating at the first degree, propagating some ideology which serves some particular interest, as the economists' doctrine of laissez faire served the interest of capitalist business."[73] Values, she believes, should be searched for openly and judged on their own merits rather than letting "commercial considerations swallow up more and more of social life, so that those who want to demand, say, improvements in the health service find it politic to point to the loss of production due to sickness and those who are concerned with education evaluate its benefits in terms of the salaries of trained personnel."[74]

In two brilliant terminal chapters, "False Prophets" and "Science and Morality," concerned with the teaching of social science, Professor Robinson chides her fellow professionals for failing to take a role of moral leadership. She writes: "The function of social science is quite different from that of the natural sciences—that is, a conception of what is the proper way to behave and the permissible pattern of relationships in family, economic and political life."[75] "There has been," she continues, "a good deal of confused controversy about the question of 'value judgments' in the social sciences. Every human being has ideological, moral and political views. To pretend to have none and to be *purely objective* must necessarily be either self-deception or a device to deceive others. . . . To eliminate value judgments from the subject-matter of social science is to eliminate the subject itself, for since it concerns human behavior it must be concerned with the value judgments that people make."[76]

Freedom and necessity today, according to Professor Robinson, require an ideology that rests on a moral philosophy which defines an accepted code of social behavior and involves more than the freedom to make money. On this note she challenges both her students and fellow social scientists as she concludes: "The economists of the laissez-faire school purported to abolish the moral problem by showing that the pursuit of self-interest by each individual rebounds to the benefit of all. The task of the generation now in rebellion is to reassert the authority of morality over technology; the business of social scientists is to help them to see both how necessary and how difficult that task is going to be."[77]

Economic Heresies (1971) is a brilliant sequel to *Freedom and Necessity,* directed, however, to a different audience. Whereas the latter dealt provocatively with topics of broad popular interest, *Economic Heresies* is an ingeniously original review of the development of economic thought. It is an economist's gold mine. In it, as indicated by its subtitle "Some Old-Fashioned Questions in Economic Theory," Professor Robinson challenges and prods her fellow economists to revise the theoretical structures of economics to fit the realities with which they purport to deal. It is as though she were responding to the first of the tasks which Beatrice Webb found challenging in 1906, that there were "two things to be done in economics, [one], a mere sweeping away of fallacies . . ."[78] as she subjects to penetrating scrutiny the sacred tenets of economic science. The result, however, proves neither as "comparatively easy" nor "futile" as Beatrice Webb forecast. Professor Robinson's own words, written in a different context, appraising a respected colleague's work, are equally appropriate here. She wrote: "It is no wonder that this book took a long time to write. It will not be read quickly. Addicts of pure economic logic who find their craving ill satisfied by the wishy-washy products peddled in contemporary journals have here a double-distilled elixir that they can enjoy, drop by drop, for many a day."[79]

Beginning with the observation that classical economic theory was founded on a set of hypothetical assumptions which supported laissez faire, free trade, the gold standard, and the profit system in a competitive free market—conditions which have long since ceased to prevail in reality—Mrs. Robinson notes that Keynes's efforts to look at the actual situation in a functioning economy backfired as his views became orthodox. "Keynes," she wrote, "was looking at the actual situation and trying to understand how an actual economy operates; he brought the argument down from timeless stationary states into the present, here and now, when the past cannot be changed and the future cannot be known. At the time it seemed like a revolution; . . . After 1945, Keynes's innovations had become orthodox in their turn; now governments had to admit that that they were concerned with maintaining the level of employment; but in respect to economic theory the old theology closed in again. . . . But once Keynes has become orthodox, the case is altered. If we are to be guaranteed near-full employment the question comes up, what form should employment take? . . . The complacency of neo-laissez faire cuts the economists off from discussing the economic problems of today just as Say's Law cut them off from discussing unemployment in the world slump."[80]

Thereafter, with intricate descriptive analysis that does not depend for its clarity on filling empty boxes with esoteric graphs, she subjects to reexamination the assumptions of each of the favorite economic models—Walras, Wicksell, Marshall, Pigou, Keynes, Harrod—and the origins of familiar economic doctrines (e.g., increasing and diminishing returns, the quantity theory, the theory of the firm, effective demand, growth analysis) and finds each, in its orthodox treatment, deficient by reason of its inability to provide understanding interpretation of present reality. For example, noting Keynes's failure to distinguish between profitable investment and socially beneficial investment, she writes: "Avoiding slumps is all to the good as far as it goes, but now there is growing up, especially in the United States, a protest against the wasteful or pernicious lines of production into which government and industry direct resources, and their failure to provide for the basic human needs of the population. The neo-neoclassical economists cannot take any part in this great debate as long as they have nothing to contribute to it except the tattered remnants of the laissez-faire doctrine that what is profitable is right."[81]

Again, after a provocative discussion of the irreversibility of technical change, she observes: "Economists have not much emphasized the opposite kind of irreversibility—the destruction of resources, the devastation of amenities, and the accumulation of poison in air and water. Pigou made a great point of 'external diseconomies' such as the smoke nuisance, but, within the confines of his stationary state, he could not emphasize *permanent* losses. It has been left rather to the natural scientists to sound the alarm, while orthodox economists, unperturbed, continue to elaborate the presumption in favor of laissez faire."[82]

She concludes by writing: "It is easy enough to make models on stated assumptions. The difficulty is to find the assumptions that are relevant to reality. . . . A model that is intended to be relevant to some actual problem must take account of the mode of operation of the economy to which it refers."[83] Instead of being content to be impeded by an outmoded theoretical scheme, she urges economists to begin again with Keynes's assumptions (a private enterprise economy facing an uncertain future, in which investment and employment decisions are made by firms in an imperfectly competitive market) and devise a model appropriate to today's capitalist industrialized nations which seek their modern goals in a setting markedly different from the setting for which Keynes wrote. Realistically ". . . modern capitalism for the last twenty-five years has been closely bound up with the armaments race and the trade in weapons (not to mention wars when they are used); it has not succeeded in overcoming poverty in its own countries, and has not succeeded in helping . . . to promote development in the Third World. Now we are told that it is in the course of making the planet uninhabitable even in peacetime. It should be the duty of economists to do their best to enlighten the public about the economic aspects of these menacing problems."[84]

The theme of *Economic Heresies* was returned to and extended by Professor Robinson in the Richard T. Ely Lecture, "The Second Crisis of Economic Theory," delivered to her fellow economists at the eighty-fourth annual meeting of the American Economic Association in December 1971.[85] Here, her main thrust was the failure of economic theory to cope with problems of the real world, specifically the unwillingness, first, to acknowledge the breakdown of *laissez faire* in the face of the problem of effective demand, and second, to deal with the problem of income distribution. "The first crisis [of economic theory] arose," she stated, "from the breakdown of a theory which could not account for the *level* of employment. The second crisis arises from a theory that cannot account for the *content* of employment. . . . Now that we all agree that government expenditures can maintain employment we should argue about what the expenditure should be for. . . . Growth in wealth is not at all the same thing as reducing poverty.[86] So long as the profession continues to accept such fictions as equilibrium, perfect competition, normality, and economic growth as an end in itself, economic theory, she warned, has been brought to near bankruptcy as ". . . economists have neglected the great problems that everyone else feels to be urgent and menacing." She challenged her profession by adding: "In short, we have not got a theory of distribution. We have nothing to say on the subject which above all others occupies the minds of the people whom economics is supposed to enlighten"[87] with the result that economists are threatened with loss of control of their subject at the hands of the politicians. At the conclusion of her address Professor Robinson received a standing ovation by an overflow audience of her fellow professionals.

The foregoing pages have traced, in a fashion too condensed to do justice to the richness and variety of her ideas, the intellectual progress of a modern economist-scholar—Adam Smith's most distinguished contemporary daughter. We have traced her course as she has moved from her demonstrated understanding of static classical economics to an awareness of the significance of the dynamic theories of Marx and Keynes, and on to such modern topics as economic growth, technical progress, international finance, income distribution, and ideological reassessment—virtually a one-woman "think tank." Professor Robinson is a thoroughgoing intellectual, dedicated to professionalism, with a strong inner committment to her own ideas. She fences herself off from anything that would be a compromise and does not seek popularity.

Her writings are often found difficult, but this is because the subjects with which she has dealt are complex and abstract. She eschews the mathematizing trend that has penetrated the social sciences, believing that a science that deals with so many unpredictable variables as economics does not benefit by being placed in a mathematical strait-jacket. Her vast knowledge of her subject and its literature is evident and she explores it with a strong, original, and determined mind.

It is significant to note that Professor Robinson is the only woman economist named in a recent study of the 101 separate contributions that have made up the 62 major accomplishments throughout the world in social sciences in this century.[88] Her teaching career has encompassed an exciting period in the development of economic science to which she has contributed notably with works that are original, penetrating, and fundamental. Mrs. Robinson is a product of the "Cambridge School" where she completed the Economics Tripos in 1925. In 1926 she married Professor E. A. G. Robinson, an eminent Cambridge economist, who was secretary of the Royal Economic Society from 1945 until 1970. She began teaching at Cambridge University in 1931 at a time when "Marshall was economics," and continued to teach for over forty years to classes of students distinguished by their multinational origins. She retired as emeritus professor of theoretical economics from the University of Cambridge in October 1971.

Throughout her many publications, apart from her profound professionalism, and her talent for penetrating analysis, Professor Robinson has displayed two fundamental qualities, viz., consistency and relevance. These qualities stand out as she pursues with almost religious fervor her search for ways to improve the teaching of theoretical economics. In an essay titled "Teaching Economics," she asks: How can we teach economic theory in order to serve the serious student attracted to the subject by humanitarian and patriotic sentiments who seeks to support economic policies that will increase human welfare? Her blueprint for doing this recommends a course of study that would be selective rather then encyclopedic, one that would stress macroeconomic theory rather than price analysis, that would integrate modern and classical economics, that would reject economic growth as an all-sufficient goal, and would cease to promote the ideology of laissez faire for the sake of symmetry. She would emphasize "that economic theory, in itself, preaches no doctrines and cannot establish any universally valid laws. It is a method of ordering ideas and formulating questions."[89] As a humane socialist she continues, with courage and conviction, to urge and prod her profession to end what she deems the current malpractice of "miseducation" in the teaching of theoretical economics, and to face up honestly to the realities of the ever-changing present. Hers is the self-adopted role of a sweeper-away of fallacies.

NOTES

1. R. K. Webb, *Harriet Martineau, A Radical Victorian* (New York: Columbia University Press, 1960), p. 366.
2. Joan Robinson, *The Economics of Imperfect Competition* (London: Macmillan & Co., Ltd., 1964), Preface V.
3. Ibid., p. 327.
4. Ibid., p. 230.
5. Ibid., p. 81.
6. Joan Robinson, *An Essay on Marxian Economics* (London: Macmillan & Co., Ltd., 1964), p. 78.
7. Joan Robinson, *Collected Economic Papers,* vol. 1 (Oxford: Basil Blackwell, 1951), Introduction VII.
8. Joan Robinson, *Economic Philosophy* (Chicago, Aldine Publishing Co., 1962), p. 104.
9. Joan Robinson, *Essays in the Theory of Employment* (Oxford: Basil Blackwell, 1953), p. 75.
10. Joan Robinson, "Kalecki and Keynes" in *Collected Economic Papers,* vol. 3 (Oxford: Basil Blackwell, 1965), p. 95.
11. Robinson, *Essay on Marxian Economics,* p. v.
12. Ibid., p. 19.
13. Ibid., p. v.
14. Joan Robinson, "Marxism: Religion and Science," *Monthly Review,* December 1962, pp. 424, 434.
15. Robinson, *Essay on Marxian Economics,* p. 22.
16. Ibid., p. 66.
17. Ibid., p. 95.

18. This essay appears also in Robinson, *Collected Economic Papers,* vol. 2 (Oxford: Basil Blackwell, 1960).

19. Joan Robinson, *The Accumulation of Capital* (London: Macmillan & Co., Ltd., 1965) 2d. ed., p. 59.

20. Ibid., p. 60.

21. Ibid., p. 60.

22. Ibid.

23. Ibid., Preface x.

24. Robinson, *The Accumulation of Capital,* p. 99.

25. Ibid.

26. Ibid.

27. Ibid., p. 173.

28. Ibid.

29. See Everett E. Hagen, *The Economics of Development* (Homewood, Ill.: Richard D. Irwin, Inc., 1968), p. 182.

30. Joan Robinson, *Exercises in Economic Analysis* (London: Macmillan & Co., Ltd., 1961), Preface V.

31. Joan Robinson, *Essays in the Theory of Economic Growth* (Oxford: Basil Blackwell, 1962), Preface V.

32. Robinson, *Economic Philosophy,* p. 81.

33. Robinson, *Essays in the Theory of Economic Growth,* Preface V.

34. Ibid., p. 17.

35. Ibid., p. 23.

36. Robinson, *Economic Philosophy,* p. 81.

37. Ibid., p. 61.

38. Robinson, *Essay on Marxian Economics,* p. 59.

39. Robinson, *Essays in the Theory of Economic Growth,* p. 26.

40. Robinson, *Economic Philosophy,* p. 82.

41. Robinson, *Essays in the Theory of Economic Growth,* pp. 98-99.

42. Ibid., p. 120.

43. Ibid., p. 132.

44. Ibid., p. 132.

45. Robinson, *Economic Philosophy,* p. 14.

46. Ibid., p. 23.

47. Robinson, *Essays in the Theory of Employment,* p. 178.

48. Robinson, *An Essay on Marxian Economics,* p. 77.

49. Robinson, *The Accumulation of Capital,* p. 33.

50. Robinson, *Economic Philosophy,* p. 4.

51. Ibid., p. 6.

52. Ibid., p. 8.

53. Ibid., p. 13.

54. Ibid., p. 26.

55. Ibid., p. 89.

56. Ibid., p. 94.

57. Ibid., p. 98.

58. Joan Robinson, *Economics: An Awkward Corner* (New York: Pantheon Books, 1967), p. 43.

59. Robinson, *Economic Philosophy,* p. 107.

60. Ibid., p. 126.

61. Ibid., p. 146.

62. Ibid., p. 124.

63. Robinson, *Economics: An Awkward Corner,* p. 3.

64. Ibid., p. 5.

65. Ibid., p. 6.

66. Ibid, p. 62.

67. Ibid., p. 83.

68. Joan Robinson, *Freedom and Necessity, An Introduction to the Study of Society* (London: George Allen and Unwin, Ltd., 1969), p. 23.

69. Ibid., pp. 60, 63.

70. Ibid., pp. 69-71.

71. Ibid., p. 87.

72. Ibid., p. 93.

73. Ibid., p. 122.

74. Ibid., p. 118.

75. Ibid., p. 120.

76. Ibid., p. 122.

77. Ibid., p. 124.

78. See above, Chap. V, n. 38.

79. Piero Sraffa, "Prelude to a Critique of Economic Theory," in Robinson, *Collected Economic Papers,* vol, 3, p. 7.

80. Joan Robinson, *Economic Heresies, Some Old-Fashioned Questions in Economic Theory* (New York: Basic Books, Inc., 1971), pp. ix, xiv, xv.

81. Ibid., pp. 50-51.

82. Ibid., p. 55.

83. Ibid., p. 141-142.

84. Ibid., pp. 143-144.

85. *The American Economic Review: Papers and Proceedings of the Eighty-fourth Annual Meeting of the American Economic Association, New Orleans, Louisiana, December 27-29, 1971.* May 1972, pp. 1-10.

86. Ibid., pp. 6 and 7.

87. Ibid., p. 9.

88. "Social Science Gains Tied to Big Teams of Scholars," *The New York Times,* March 16, 1971, p. 26.

89. "Teaching Economics," in Robinson, *Collected Economic Papers,* vol. 3, p. 5.

Postscript

> "Fellow-mammals, fellow-vertebrates, fellow-humans, I thank you. Little did my dear parents think, when they told me to stand on my own two feet, that I'd arrive at this place."
> —Thornton Wilder, *The Skin of Our Teeth*

Here, then, is the record of six women who learned to stand on their own two feet. It is a record of a select company, an omitted chapter in the treatises on the history of economics. It has been an attempt to bring out of limbo the records of these spiritual daughters and granddaughters of Adam Smith who made distinguished individual contributions toward expanding the area of economic understanding, and whose works provide a worthy obbligato to the works of Adam Smith's sons. Their careers demonstrate that economics is a profession that women can handle as well as men.

Unlike others of their sex, each of these six was exceptional in her unwillingness merely to be an onlooker or silent partner of the economic scene. Each made a singular contribution to the development of political economy. It is noteworthy that their ideas, dating from the early nineteenth century to the present, not only parallel and reflect the ideology of their time but fall into a pattern whereby each foretells the course that economic science was yet to take. Their interests foreshadowed a number of later developments which have occupied economists to the present. Indeed, a capsule version of the history of economic thought is implicit in the careers and contributions of these women. Through their writings can be traced the intellectual movement in economics from the rich but diffuse state in which it had been left by

Adam Smith, through the Ricardian era, through Marxism, Marshall, and welfare economics, to the tightly knit and multifaceted discipline it is today.

Viewing their six careers in perspective, the observer sees in the composite the advancing dialogue which has characterized the last two centuries of social thought and action. The debate of these women has been, not with each other, nor with their fellow professionals, but—a debate between individualism and social responsibility. The judgment of history cannot be hurried and the outcome has yet to be determined, but each, from Jane Marcet to Joan Robinson, caught the tempo of her own era as she sought the welfare of society and gave emphasis to moral principles of social behavior.

In the light of their successful independence the question inevitably arises: Why have there been so few women economists? The question is not an easy one to answer. Economics is abstract, it is analytical, it is controversial. As women have sought escape from kitchen and sweatshop, they have found no open doors welcoming them to those areas of activity traditionally occupied by men. While none of these difficulties is insuperable, it must be acknowledged that economics is an arduous profession. It is not a subject which, once learned, is forever mastered. Not only is it ever changing, but, with the increasing complexity of society, the discipline itself becomes more complex. Neither is it a subject which can be studied, put aside for marriage and a family, and returned to with ease years later. Economics is a hard taskmaster; it can require a lifetime of concentration to reveal its insights. As though these hurdles were not sufficient, modern economics also requires a high degree of mathematical competence, a skill in which many women regrettably feel frail. Here the vicious circle of reasoning that women were so unlikely to make use of mathematics that they should not have to trouble their heads to learn it has meant that they have often been shortchanged in gaining instruction in this universal language in their early education. Calculus and linear algebra are essential equipment for modern economists, and one to two years of advanced mathematics are required for entrance to nearly all major graduate schools. It is not inaccurate to say that a career in economics requires expertness in two professions.

Despite these exacting professional demands, the number of women economists is increasing. Women are now pursuing careers and distinguishing themselves by combining economics with education, journalism, business and finance, labor relations, government service, ecology, and politics. As we see the world being transformed by applications of technology, new visions of social relations, and an all but overwhelming array of social problems—overpopulation, rapacious depletion of natural resources, environmental deterioration, poverty, war—it is appropriate that women, trained in economics, should tackle these problems, which affect women's lives no less than men's. Women must be given the opportunity to apply their special talents, vision and creativeness, to help choose our social priorities and to seek solutions for our social ills. Six of Adam Smith's daughters have shown the way. It remains for their successors to respond with similar intellectual sensitivity to the longer vision of social needs and to share in determining the course that society will take.

Index

Biographical references to the six economists discussed in individual chapters in this book are given only when they occur in a chapter other than that devoted to the economist cited.